14445
V94

PAUL B. WESTON

Chairman, Department of Police Science
Sacramento State College

Criminal
Justice
and Law Enforcement:
Cases

Prentice-Hall, Inc., Englewood Cliffs, New Jersey

Illustrations in this book are by William Durston, Sacramento State College.

ISBN: 0–13–193367–1

Library of Congress Catalog Card Number: 73–37636

10 9 8 7 6 5 4 3 2 1

PRINTED IN THE UNITED STATES OF AMERICA

Prentice-Hall International, Inc., *London*

Prentice-Hall of Australia Pty. Ltd., *Sydney*

Prentice-Hall of Canada, Ltd., *Toronto*

Prentice-Hall of India Private Limited, *New Delhi*

Prentice-Hall of Japan, Inc., *Tokyo*

Contents

Introduction

The case study method of instruction facilitates learning by linking case content and textbook topics and by encouraging the exchange of opinions and viewpoints among students during discussion sessions. The case studies in this book are designed to contribute to this type of learning process. Each case provides factual information that is likely to promote analysis and discussion and thus aid in developing a student's ability to analyze, evaluate, and reason.

The cases presented will supplement any of the available texts likely to be adopted in introductory college-level courses in police science, law enforcement, or criminal justice. The major issue involved in many of these cases can be related to single chapters of these textbooks. Other cases with a broader focus can be related to two or more chapters in these books.

The areas for analysis and discussion provided by these case studies range from perception of the issue, through the dimensions of the problem, to alternative solutions. The topic of discussion is focused by the facts of each case study, but the scope of the discussion is limited only by the range of student opinions and ideas.

Some cases are presented in straight narrative style, while others are written in dialogue form as the best means of joining the personalities and the situations of a case study. In some of the cases written in dialogue form, only one or two major characters are emphasized for simplicity and coherence, although more personalities may have been involved in the case. The raw data was "the story"; the treatment was the author's decision on "how to tell the story."

Each case presents a situation or episode experienced by real people at some time in the past. There has been no "doctoring" to develop points, theories, or problems. Names have been changed in some cases to avoid embarrassing any persons or their families. The locale of other cases has been masked to avoid any geographical identification unsuited to the analysis of the case. The year of occurrence has been omitted as a general rule if "dating" the case was undesirable. Continuity in such cases has been preserved by identifying the days of the week and the date of the month. In any case, facts have only been altered to provide a better balance between the event and the characters.

Each chapter contains two or more related case studies oriented to the chapter topic. Chapters begin with an introduction presenting the major issue of the case studies that follow. A summary section at the end of each chapter reviews the relationship of each case study to the major issue.

In using this casebook, students should first read a case for content. Then, in a review reading, students should plot out all the information about the major event and its circumstances, and the interrelationships between the characters in the case and the event. Then, as a third step, students can sum up as precisely as possible the issue and problems presented in a case. Lastly, students should use their perceptions of the dimensions of the issue and the problems of the case to form their own judgments about the issue involved, and to formulate some possible alternative solutions.

There is a series of questions at the end of each case study. These questions probe the major and subordinate issues in each case study and serve to structure analysis and discussion. There are no "key" answers to these questions. Inherent in the case method of study is the expectation that students will differ as to the "correct" answer to questions probing and prying into the facts of a case. The value of these cases and this method of learning is that students are forced into a decision-making analysis and justification of their decision on the basis of their perceptions and evaluation of the event and the people in a case study.

PAUL B. WESTON

CHAPTER ONE

Community Control of Police Behavior

In the early years of law enforcement, there was considerable public support for the concept of a force of police who would attempt to prevent crime, arrest known offenders of crimes not prevented, and investigate crimes in which the offenders were unknown so as to identify them for the purpose of arrest and prosecution.

Public opinion assumed that police and police powers were very necessary for the protection of life and property and the maintenance of peace and tranquility. Over many years, communities developed their police forces in response to these views.

The American model of police services at local levels has its origin in the British, rather than European, police organizations. British police were organized to serve individual communities and were responsible to local government. French, German, and Italian police were organized nationally and responsible to a central government.

The British system of policing communities has its origin in the "Watch" of citizens who provided basic police protection to safeguard their own and their neighbors' property. The need for police services, plus the inconvenience of serving "watch duty," led to hiring "Constables" to supplement or replace the local "Watch." In 1829, the needs of England's major city, London, led to the concept of municipal policing.

A national police would be repugnant to the principle of a division of powers and functions between federal and state governments. The U.S. Constitution divided powers between the central government and the governments of the several states. The powers of the central government are enumerated, and the powers not delegated to the central government are reserved for the states or the people. Five of the early amendments to the Constitution safeguarded the rights of persons accused of crime, restricting the law-enforcement powers of both the central government and the state governments. One of the major features of our federal system is that neither national nor state government is inferior to the other, or in conflict with the other, in the ordinary operations of government.[1] In addition, the economics of the new country suggest that the need for national police services was subordinated to more essential central government needs. In any event, the speed and scope of the westward expansion would have made it difficult for any central government to provide police services to frontier settlements.

Thus, the responsibility for organizing police and funding them has fallen upon local government at the municipal and county level.[2] Local control of police organizations has developed a fragmented national non-system of policing noted for its thousands of autonomous and independent police departments subject to no overall administrative supervision or control.

Governments at city, county, and state levels have struggled with the problem of controlling police and their law enforcement services. In some localities, the basic motivation to exercise control over police behavior is "political" rather than a desire to improve the quality of police services or to upgrade police officers and their role in law enforcement. In other areas, control at executive levels of a police force may be the only means of wiping out long-standing corrupt practices and low standards of work performance.

The three cases in this chapter array people who disagree and the circumstances of disagreement. The issue in each case is the control of police behavior.[3] The first two cases detail the removal of police chiefs. Case Study 1 is concerned with the years prior to the Civil War, while Case Study 2 is more recent. Since over one hundred years separate the dates of the dismissals of the police chief in these two cases, the similarity of the circumstances certainly suggests the continuity of this problem of the control of police behavior.[4] The last case is related to a means of controlling police behavior when local police services are substandard—a well-motivated citizen is placed in charge of the reform of a police unit.

---

[1]Arthur C. Millspaugh, *Crime Control by the National Government* (Washington, D.C.: The Brookings Institution, 1937), pp. 43–59.

[2]James Q. Wilson, *Varieties of Police Behavior* (Cambridge, Mass.: Harvard University Press, 1969), pp. 4–15.

[3]The President's Commission on Law Enforcement and Administration of Justice, *Task Force Report: The Police* (Washington, D.C.: Government Printing Office, 1967), pp. 30–35.

[4]Bruce Smith, *Police Systems in the United States* (2nd rev. ed.), ed. Bruce Smith, Jr. (New York: Harper & Row, 1960), pp. 1–9.

Boston and City Marshal Francis Tukey

The Night Watch was established in Boston in 1836 to provide police services during the hours of darkness. Burglars and thieves looted stores, piers, and warehouses in the night-time, and robbers used the natural cover of darkness as an aid in surprising their victims and in escaping pursuit. The mission of the Night Watch was patrol. Watchmen were to walk their rounds slowly and silently and, now and then, stand still and listen, and also take appropriate action to prevent crime and arrest offenders. Two years later, in 1838, Boston established a day police force of six men, independent of the Night Watch, to provide the growing city with around-the-clock police services. The work of the Night Watch over a two-year period had been approved by the community, and a similar daytime patrol was a natural extension of police services.

A new mayor, elected in 1845, was elected on a "Reform" pledge to improve municipal government and it services to the people of Boston. He committed his administration to enlarge the police services of Boston in order to cope with the growing problem of crime and disorders in the streets. Boston was a growing city, and the amount of crime kept pace with the increase in population. The new Mayor promptly appointed Francis Tukey to direct the municipality's expanding public safety enterprise. Tukey was named "City Marshal" and provided with funds for the appointment of eighteen new patrolmen and three detectives.[5]

Francis Tukey was born in Maine in 1814. Employed initially as a

[5]Roger Lane, *Policing The City: Boston 1822–1855* (Cambridge, Mass.: Harvard University Press, 1967), pp. 15–45.

FIGURE 1 Francis Tukey, City Marshal of Boston. Tukey originated the police lineup and was the first police official to arm local police beyond the traditional police "baton," providing military swords to Boston's police for riot duty.

mechanic, Tukey went to law school and became involved with Boston politics. He was a huge man with curly hair and a heavy, hard face. He was not of the Puritan aristocracy and he lacked the family connections useful in Colonial politics. However, he made up for these handicaps by harnessing a driving energy to his day's work. He finished the study of law in less than two years and impressed his friends with his ability to get work done. Illustrative of the known capacity of Tukey for accomplishment is the fact that at the time of his appointment as City Marshal, the City Council voted funds to more than double the new police unit so that Tukey could not only provide day-time police services but also supplement the Night Watch and begin the formation of a new investigative division. An analysis of Tukey's stewardship of police services in Boston indicates his objectives were deterring crime, controlling public disorder, and apprehending criminals and making cases against them.

Marshal Tukey waged an uncompromising war against prostitution, gambling, and drunkenness. It was a planned campaign ranging from the licensing of theatres and their supervision by police to massive raids. In one raid, an entire street known to be the area in which prostitutes and gamblers congregated and carried out their various business pursuits was blocked off and officers assigned to raid each individual residence or place of business. A total of 60 men and 90 women were arrested in this raid and prosecuted on a variety of minor charges of crime against the good order of the City of Boston.

Tukey selected his detectives on the basis of their skills in criminal investigation. At that time, a successful detective solved cases by his knowledge of criminals and their *modus operandi*. Burglars, forgers, counterfeiters, and boarding-house thieves were a major problem for the investigative unit as these criminals were not usually apprehended during their operations.

An innovative procedure developed by Marshal Tukey was the "show-up"—an early version of the present-day "line up." Since a police patrolman's role was to deter crime as well as to arrest offenders, a detective's ability to perform in his assigned role was enhanced by a knowledge of criminals. In Tukey's show-up, the police who would patrol and the detectives who would investigate were the "audience," and known criminals were the "actors." The procedure was designed to identify criminals to police attending the show-up session. The number of persons presented for inspection by the police varied, but Tukey had a good supply of "talent" for these shows: persons legally arrested and "shown" prior to their appearance in court, and persons suspected of crime and being investigated by police. Some of the police officers were advised by Tukey to bring along victims and witnesses in pending cases, to view the suspicious persons for the purpose of identifying offenders.

Tukey used mass arrests, such as those that he used to clean up prostitution and gambling, in a modified form to correct other municipal problems related to police services for the growing city. For example, during the winter of 1848, after a particular heavy snow storm, 91 persons were arrested for failure to clear the snow and ice from their sidewalks; and on April 21, 1851, a total of 101 persons were arrested for keeping unlicensed dogs and for other violations related to dogs. Tukey's police did not have the power to cite or summons these lesser offenders, and an arrest was a physical taking of the offender and a walk or carriage ride to court or place of detention.

An unforseen problem for Boston and its city police developed because of the potato famine in Ireland from 1846 to 1852. Irish immigration peaked throughout the Colonies during Tukey's years as police executive, and Boston as a prosperous city of opportunity became a popular port for Irish immigrants. The newcomers lacked economic resources, and their arrival brought a new dimension to police problems in Boston. Marshal Tukey and his police worked to resolve the Irish problem in Boston by various acts of emergency relief and participation in municipal charity plans for the benefit of the poor.

During Tukey's years as City Marshal, the vast majority of arrested criminals were of Irish birth. Marshal Tukey noted in his 1851 report to the City Council, and the people of Boston, that he was not bitter against persons of Irish birth, but that he was bitter about the poverty of these immigrants and their plight in being unable to find gainful occupations in Boston.

The rise of the Irish immigrants from the ranks of common labor to positions in government presented Marshal Tukey with his first major problem. By 1850, about 35,000 of the city's population of 136,000 were of Irish birth, and the "Irish Democrats" were a balance-of-power splinter group in Boston politics. In June of 1851, the Irish power structure in Boston proposed that the City Council add an Irishman to the police force. Barney McGinniskin was nominated. A number of Boston businessmen signed a petition to the City Council pleading for his appointment. McGinniskin was appointed to the police force and reported for work. but Marshal Tukey refused to assign him to police duty. In a press release, Tukey stated that applicants for the police force were normally above the level of common laborers, and that it was now a well-paying occupation that drew applicants from among the ranks of artisans, mechanics, clerks, and bookkeepers. Tukey's specific reason for rejecting McGinniskin was that he was a cabman who worked in an area frequented by prostitutes and gamblers, and he had a criminal record. McGinniskin had been convicted of rioting several years prior to his application for the police position. The Mayor refused to become involved with Tukey's denial of McGinniskin's appointment. He was in the middle of a campaign for reelection, and refusal to assign McGinniskin became a political issue in the mayoralty election. The people of Boston, including a considerable number of Irish voters, went to the polls and a new mayor was elected. He promptly ordered Tukey to assign McGinniskin to active police work.

Boston's experience with Marshal Tukey, its first tough policeman, was highlighted by the controversy about his cooperation with Federal authorities in enforcing the provisions of the Fugitive Slave Law. The first major criticism of Tukey's role concerned the behavior of the police during a meeting of abolitionists at Faneuil Hall in 1850. The gathering was a protest against the Fugitive Slave Law and its enforcement in Massachusetts, and it was broken up by a disorderly invasion of local toughs. Tukey was in command of a small group of police, but according to the abolitionists, he failed to take appropriate action. After a hearing, however, the City Council refused to rebuke Tukey.

Another major criticism of Tukey and his police arose from his conduct in the case of Thomas Sims, a fugitive slave. The United States Marshal in Boston received an arrest warrant for the seventeen-year-old runaway slave, and asked for local police help in serving it. Tukey passed the warrant on to two of his experienced officers, and they arrested Sims a few days later. Sims was informed he was a suspect in a burglary case, but suspecting the true reason, he resisted arrest and stabbed one of the arresting officers with a knife. He was subdued, taken into custody, and imprisoned in a special cell on the third floor of the Boston courthouse. In defending his role in the arrest, Tukey claimed that his men were better able to find and arrest Sims than untrained and inexperienced federal officers, that Sims' arrest had been made with only reasonable force and without disorder, and that his men had been "employed" by the United States Marshal for this purpose.

For nine days, Marshal Tukey assigned every available man he could spare to surround the courthouse and cooperate with federal authorities in preventing the rescue of Sims by the Boston Vigilance Committee, an aggressive group of abolitionists.

Tukey, a practical man, utilized a police barricade procedure for the security of the courthouse. Unfortunately, the heavy chain he had placed around the courthouse and its massive supporting pillars had a symbolism to the abolitionists: chains and slavery.

The Boston Vigilance Committee denounced the police as "Slave Catchers" and "Kidnappers," and posted the residential areas in which slaves found refuge with warnings addressed to the Black population: "You are hereby respectfully cautioned and advised to avoid conversing with the Watchmen and Police Officers of Boston."

Also denounced by this abolitionist group, and the subject of a later official review by the Massachusetts Senate, was Marshal Tukey's arming of the Boston police with swords provided from the U.S. Military stores in Boston. Tukey admitted at the Senate hearing that he knew he was violating state law in thus arming his police beyond their traditional night stick or truncheon, but he stated that his action was designed to prevent disorder while Sims was in custody, and while the slave was being transported to the harbor and the ship which would take him back to his owners in South Carolina.

Tukey and his police did not reduce the amount of crime in Boston during his years of police leadership. These were difficult days for law enforcement in this major seaport of New England. It was becoming a center for the import and export of merchandise, and its large increase in population was weighted with persons of lower socioeconomic standing. Tukey was given credit by knowledgeable citizens, however, for the control of crime. He was credited with preventing the spiraling increase in crime that one might expect because of the increasing number of local citizenry living at poverty levels, and the increasing amount of merchandise brought to,

FIGURE 2 A contingent of Tukey's Boston police prepared for riot duty. The majority are armed with swords.

stored in, and shipped from Boston. Illustrative of the esteem which the business community of Boston held for Tukey, was his selection by the Bankers Association of New England as chairman of a group formed to combat forgeries, counterfeiting and bank frauds.

But in April 1852 the municipal administration cut back the City Marshal's authority by establishing annual terms of employment for the city police, thus revoking Tukey's rule of tenure for police officers for "good behavior." Then, in June 1852, a new police ordinance reaffirmed the policy of annual police appointments, and revoked the title of City Marshal—assigning the marshal's function and duties to a new position: Chief of Police.

Tukey fought this technique of dismissal, claiming that it was nothing but "cold politics." His friends in Boston's government cited the similarity between the job of "City Marshal" and the new position of "Police Chief," and that Tukey's performance as City Marshal made him the man best qualified for the job of "Police Chief."

A month later, in July 1852, Tukey's employment as City Marshal was terminated. His request for a public hearing was denied, and a former City Councilman was named the new Chief of Police for the city of Boston.

QUESTIONS

1. Was the termination (dismissal) of Francis Tukey as police executive of the City of Boston justified?

2. Was the criticism of Tukey by the Boston Vigilance Committee for his action in the fugitive slave case a proper factor to be considered in his dismissal?

3. Was the arming of police with swords by Tukey justified by the circumstances?

4. Was Tukey's rejection of McGinniskin, an Irish applicant for police employment, a proper factor to weigh in considering Tukey's dismissal?

5. Was Tukey's innovative action in developing the police "show-up" a factor in his dismissal?

6. Was Tukey's technique of mass "raids" and arrests to reduce prostitution justified?

7. Was Tukey's use of the police power of summary arrests for minor offenses, such as failure to secure a dog license or to clean sidewalks of snow and ice, a factor that should have contributed to the decision to dismiss him?

The City Manager Fires
the Police Chief

This is a case study of community control of police behavior in 1970. The city involved is an ordinary one, its size is not important, though it is a large city with an interesting history.

In 1961, a management survey of the police department in this city stated there was no reasoned preference for either a professional or nonprofessional as Police Chief, noting that a study of over fifty years incumbency in this office revealed nothing more than the fact that professional and nonprofessional appointees have failed in about equal proportions. In their fifty-year review of police leadership, the survey analysts found that only two Police Chiefs had served for five years or more. In its recommendations, this survey report sought tenure, or at least a five-year term of office, for the Police Chief, saying that a brief tenure of police leadership was not in harmony with the goal of improving the department and providing executive guidance for its growth and development. Municipal government in this city was marked by its hard line of politics-as-usual, and no action was taken on the police survey report. In 1968, a police scandal resulted in an investigation by the District Attorney, and the conviction of two detectives and four officers for accepting bribes from known gamblers so that gambling operations would have immunity from the police. In 1969, the good people of the community took over in a drive for reform. At a special election in November 1969, the voters approved a new City Charter calling for a city manager type of government.

This case study uses only two main characters to tell the story, the City Manager and the Police Chief. A "narrator" is used as a device to fill in gaps in the story without introducing other characters. In this fashion, the basic conflict is heightened by the one-to-one opposition. The first two scenes are set in the City Council Chamber and set the stage for the forth-coming conflict. Scene 3 is set in the Police Auditorium, and—appropri-ately—details what will become Chief Leonard's position or viewpoint. Scenes 4 through 7 are set in the office of the City Manager because each scene is another "count" in the countdown leading to the dismissal of Chief Leonard by the City Manager. In all, the case spans about one-and-a-half years.

CAST OF CHARACTERS

City Manager	THOMAS J. SCHMIDT
Police Chief	BENJAMIN LEONARD
Narrator	ANONYMOUS OBSERVER

SCENE 1: *City Council Chamber.*

NARRATOR: The police department had the unfortunate reputation of be-ing a part of the political system of the city. The new City Charter at-tempted to divorce the management of the police function from local politics by providing for the appointment of the Police Chief by the City Manager, who was a career public official; and by allowing only the City Manager to remove the Police Chief, after an adequate show-ing of cause for such termination.

The new City Charter was effective January 1, 1970. The Police Chief, who had survived the 1968–69 scandal, retired at 12:01 mid-night, the day the new Charter went into effect. A month later, on Feb-ruary 2, the new City Manager was appointed.

Thomas J. Schmidt was the new City Manager. He had been an Assistant City Manager in a large city in Texas. Schmidt, at the time of his appointment, was 45 years of age, had been a Romance Language major at a good university in New England, and had gone on to com-plete law school; but he never practiced law because of his interest in public administration.

When he accepted the earlier Texas appointment, Schmidt had served sixteen years with the United States Government, as an intern and then as an administrator, in a progressively successful career. He was a tall and heavy man, 6 feet 3 inches in height, and about 230 pounds. He had grey hair and a bit of it always seemed to hang over his forehead. He wore steel-rimmed glasses, which always seemed to slide down to the end of his nose. When he talked, one hand or the other was always in motion, pushing back his hair, or his glasses.

In his first appearance before the City Council the new City Manager thanked the Council for his appointment and said:

This is my pledge to the City Council and also the people of this city: I pledge to you a government dedicated to the best interests of all the people. This will always be my exclusive consideration. I shall favor no special groups. I shall work and fight solely for the best welfare of all the people. In this effort, I hope I may have your continued support.

On March 1, scarcely a month later, the City Manager announced he would appoint the new Police Chief at 8 A.M. the next day, at the opening of the City Council session. Thomas J. Schmidt was a City Manager who appeared to know the public relations value of a few well-chosen words.

Now, in his first major public statement since accepting the new post of City Manager, Schmidt tells the people of the city and the City Council who the new Police Chief will be.

CITY MANAGER SCHMIDT: Many policemen in this city have given their lives so that others may live in security and peace. The nobility of these men, and that sense of dedication which caused them to lay down their lives, is a source of great pride to everyone. We are proud of these police heroes and proud of our Police Department, and we are equally proud to announce the appointment of one of our own police to the position of Chief.

Your new Chief is an up-from-the-ranks professional police officer, self-educated while a policeman, and a graduate of the FBI National Police Academy. He is a family man, a religious man, and an honest man; and I know he will be a credit to this city, and to the fine men and women of the Police Department. Now, by the power vested in me as City Manager by the City Charter, I hereby appoint Benjamin Leonard Chief of Police. (*The new Chief rises from a front row chair and joins the City Manager.*) Raise your right hand. (*New Chief raises his hand.*) Do you solemnly swear that you will perform all the . . . (*fade out*).

NARRATOR: The new chief, Benjamin Leonard, was about five years older than the city manager—about fifty. He was a few inches shorter and not too many pounds lighter. He was a grey man—grey eyes, grey hair, and a greyish complexion. The new chief had started out in his adult life as a warehouseman at the local Air Force Base, moved up to clerical work, and at twenty-four became a policeman.

On the police force, he had worked in patrol, traffic and detectives; and while going to college and law school at night, he had been assigned to the Civil Defense Unit, a day-work assignment which permitted him to attend night school. He had been number 1 on the sergeant's list, number 8 on the lieutenant's list, and number 2 on the captain's list.

Where Schmidt, the new City Manager, was a man of good spirits with an apparent sense of humor, Chief Leonard was without humor, reserved, and suspicious. Shortly after being sworn in, he was asked to say a few words. After thanking the City Manager for selecting him as the new Chief, he faced the City Council and the others in the room and talked of his new job.

POLICE CHIEF LEONARD: I have accepted this appointment with the understanding that the Police Department is underpaid and undermanned, and that working conditions should be improved to bring the Department up from the low point it has fallen in the public esteem. I will devote myself, night and day, unceasingly, in a great and all-out effort to improve police salaries and working conditions, and to provide sufficient men and women in the Police Department for the protection of our city. I look for magnificent support from within our Department; and I believe we will earn magnificent public support. I thank all of you for your confidence in me and in my record in the Police Department.

NARRATOR: In a few last-minute words, City Manager Schmidt vowed to "clean the politics out of the Police Department" and he promised the new Chief that he would be allowed to operate free of political or partisan interference in the day-to-day management of police operations. Things looked good for the Police Department.

SCENE 2:   *The City Council Chamber.*
TIME: *30 days later.*

NARRATOR: On April 1, and it wasn't an April Fool's joke, Chief Leonard announced the biggest shake-up in years. He termed it "Operation Efficiency," and said that the transfers followed accepted modern management patterns in the elimination of policemen from clerical positions, the replacement of male personnel in the courts with women, and the discontinuance of the Traffic Division. It was a reasonable starting action for the new Chief. However, the City Manager asked the Chief to appear before the City Council with him to justify the action.

POLICE CHIEF LEONARD: Gentlemen, the situation on which I based my executive action is a local crisis in crime. The need for increasing the size of the Police Department is urgent, but budget funds are not available. With this action, I have placed more men in the field, and kept within our limited budget, by taking men from desk jobs and by abolishing the Traffic Division. The Police Department gains more men for the actual crime-stopping work of the police. The discontinuance of the

Traffic Division is only temporary, and I will reestablish it in some modified form just as soon as the Department has enough men to discharge its primary function of preserving the public peace and protecting life and property from the criminals who are making the streets of the city unsafe for its citizens.

CITY MANAGER: Gentlemen, the Police Chief was appointed to run the Police Department. I think he has hit the right note in management when he takes this kind of action on the grounds that he can find more useful work for these men elsewhere in the operations of his Department. Now, as to the claim that the Department is short-handed—this is something that we must study, and that will take time.

SCENE 3: *The City Police Auditorium.*
TIME: *Two months later.*

NARRATOR: Almost ninety days went by quietly. Chief Leonard made several presentations to the City Council about his Department being short-handed and requested a larger budget. He received little encouragement. Then, the Grand Jury was asked to investigate a budding city scandal involving the city's redevelopment project. One of the contracting firms tearing down buildings for redevelopment construction claimed that previously "acceptable" payments to local inspectors of Buildings and Housing had been restructured to include payments to Fire, Police, and Air Pollution representatives. It was all kept pretty quiet. The first outburst came from Chief Leonard. He assembled all of his ranking superior officers in the Police Auditorium, sending out an order directing them to report to headquarters for the promotion of new superiors. After making the promotions, the Chief spoke to the assembled police "brass."

POLICE CHIEF LEONARD: It is appropriate at this time to state that the work we do requires the very highest ethical standards, and it is on this subject that I want to talk to you newly promoted officers today, and to the other ranking officers who are here today. I think it is timely and desirable for me to talk to the higher ranks, and through them to the entire department, on the subject of police corruption—and I shall mince no words.

Corruption exists in the Police Department—our Department, but it must and will be rooted out. We have men and women who have not hesitated to sell us all out for a few dollars. We have traitors. We have people who have not only degraded themselves—for which they will some day answer in the sight of Almighty God—but, these people have also attempted to destroy what we are trying to do for this Department. Gentlemen, it will not go on. If I have to tear down and rebuild this entire Department, it will not go on—and let that be understood! Remember that, gentlemen, and thank you.

NARRATOR: Chief Leonard was talking about the basic responsibility of supervisors. He told his listening officers, and they were listening I'm sure, that he would hold them responsible for corrupt acts on the part of the men and women assigned to them. He was insisting that the supervisors shoulder their responsibility to prevent any dishonest acts. It is not an unusual charge to make to a group of supervisors; but the local reporters were now in the habit of running to the City Manager for comment. Chief Leonard had not cleared his actions with City Manager Schmidt, nor was Schmidt at the promotion ceremonies. He may have been at the Grand Jury hearing. In any event, when the reporters found him, he didn't fly off the handle, he responded quietly to their questions.

SCENE 4: *Office of the City Manager.*
TIME: *Later the same day.*

CITY MANAGER: The substance of Chief Leonard's remarks can be true of any city employee. That is, the city as an employer adheres to the principle that an oath of office is sacred and that the men, women, and children who live or work in our city are entitled to honor and decency in any city employee. Any city employee has a basic responsibility to conduct himself with honor, decency and integrity. Gentlemen, I'm sure that the Grand Jury, through its current investigation, will make certain that this principle is followed by taking appropriate action where any city employee has violated his oath of office. In the past, disciplinary action has been taken only against the guilty individuals themselves. Usually, outright expulsion would be in order when the charges were as serious as those suggested by the complainant in this case—the demolition firm in the Redevelopment Project. Now, I will have to ask Chief Leonard for more information about the implied threat of expulsion or demotion of ranking officers which he included in his warning to the entire Police Department. You gentlemen of the press know, I hope, that I do not interfere with department heads. As City Manager, I only participate in the affairs of a Department when it is necessary to give that department, and its head, any necessary direction and guidance on policies and procedures. Thank you.

SCENE 5: *City Manager's Office.*
TIME: *About a year after the Police Auditorium incident.*

NARRATOR: In the next twelve months, more and more friction developed between Chief Leonard, his men, and the City Manager. Right after the

Labor Day weekend, Chief Leonard was again in the news, and again in a controversy. This time it was because he had abruptly transferred a Court Bailiff to duty at the city jail. It was a summary and a punitive transfer, telephoned by the Chief's secretary to the Sergeant in charge of the City Court detail, and it was to take effect "forthwith"—immediately. The summary transfer issue began one day when the good Chief came into his office, was presented with the morning papers by his secretary, and saw on page 2 of the local morning paper a picture of a policeman in uniform holding an umbrella over a retiring City Judge to shield him from a mild rain. John Marquez, a senior policeman assigned for years to the city courts, was the offending officer. "Poor judgment," the Chief said. His idea of proper police duty did not include playing footman to official dignitaries. And that was that. For ten days. Ten days in which the City Manager and the just-retired judge refused any comment on the chief's abrupt action.

Ten days later, Chief Leonard admitted that the officer was not entirely to blame, saying the press photographer had stated that he had asked the officer to step into the picture in the umbrella-holding role to give the picture of the judge some action. The Chief also admitted that Marquez had been on his own time, his lunch break, when the picture was taken. Marquez, Chief Leonard announced, was being transferred out of the city jail assignment and back to patrol duty, which had been his assignment prior to his service at the city courts. When asked when Marquez would be restored to his court duty, Chief Leonard said that was a matter to be considered at a later date, and that any decision would be made without regard for outside pressure.

The umbrella issue was followed by other incidents. Chief Leonard succeeded in antagonizing nearly everybody from the city manager to his own officers. He had the personality of a blunt instrument and was uninhibited by tact or diplomacy. But the people of the city—and their city manager—accepted him during that first year because he had a simple goal of establishing the policeman as a professional, and the Police Department as a professional organization.

About a year after his appointment, Chief Leonard began to discover that the city's economy and the labor market were operating against his attempt to get a better class of police recruit. The city was paying an entrance salary not much above day-laborer wages and expecting a college-level potential from its applicants. Additionally, the low city pay forced most of the city employees to "moonlight," to seek work in their off-duty hours for private employers, in order to add a few dollars to their city salaries. The police were no different from other city employees; they mixed concrete or drinks, or anything else, to add to their meager police pay.

This was offensive to the Chief's personal dream of the policeman becoming a true professional through self-improvement studies while off-duty. He began a campaign to cut down on outside employment, forbidding more and more types of employment for police, and requiring prior approval of the Chief before accepting any off-duty jobs.

The Police Department was near mutiny. There had been other times during the previous year when Chief Leonard had rubbed some one or some group in the Department the wrong way and earned a sharp response, but he had turned it away with a casual you-do-your-job-and-I'll-do-mine attitude. Now, perhaps, he had gone too far. What had been refreshing independence in his first year as Chief had become an inconvenient resistance to accommodation.

The city manager refused to comment to the press about the "moonlighting" issue; but when a new controversy arose, about a recent promotion within the Department, the city manager asked Chief Leonard to come down to his office. Here they are:

CITY MANAGER: Chief, I asked you to come over to give me the facts, your own rationale on this promotion mess—

POLICE CHIEF: (*Interrupting*) It is *not* a mess.

CITY MANAGER: Alright, Ben, have it your own way, but you passed over a man. I know, and you know, that you could pick out any one of the first three men on the list for the lieutenant's vacancy, but it is a reversal of past practices, and that's what I want to find out about: why you appointed the number-two lieutenant.

POLICE CHIEF: I had a letter advocating an early promotion for the number-one man. It was written by a respectable business man, but I cannot let anyone say that he has influenced the police chief.

CITY MANAGER: The man you passed over—did he ask this man to write the letter?

POLICE CHIEF: The business man claimed the idea originated with him, but that is immaterial. The idea is that no one can say that they influenced the chief.

SCENE 6:   *Office of the City Manager.*
TIME: *Three weeks later.*

NARRATOR: The next public conflict between Chief Leonard and the City Manager appeared to have its roots in the growing use of drugs by youngsters and the development of a local therapy group, Mid-House Associates—a privately financed attempt to try to help youngsters on drugs without arresting them. The group asked the Chief to send over a Police Department expert on juveniles and drug use as a speaker, and he refused. Again, the City Manager called Chief Leonard to his office.

CITY MANAGER: Ben, sit down. I'm sorry to get you away from a busy schedule, but I'm upset about this lack of cooperation with Mid-House, the drug-abuse people. They are trying to do good, in fact, to help you —the police.

POLICE CHIEF (*Interrupting*):   We don't need their help. Drug use has a contagion factor and the youngsters are meeting hard-core "junkies" over there. Its becoming a market place for all kinds of drugs. Half of the staff are MD's and nurses, and some of them were involved with drugs. They get no police speaker.

SCENE 7:   *Office of the City Manager.*
TIME: *A month after the Mid-House incident.*

NARRATOR: The pattern of conflict between the Chief and the City Manager continued. A police intelligence unit had been one of Chief Leonard's innovations, and its commanding officer, a sergeant, testified before the Senate Internal Security Subcommittee in Washington. His testimony identified him as an undercover agent who had infiltrated the local Black Panther organization. The City Manager told the Chief he might have had good reason for his action, but why didn't he confer with someone before approving this Washington testimony? Chief Leonard said that the federal government had asked for his cooperation, and that he had not hestitated to cooperate. The City Manager told Chief Leonard: "Okay, that may be true, but you heard what some of the blasts have been in the paper. One was 'A Return to McCarthyism.' " The Police Chief's response was: "That shouldn't bother you."

At about the same time, a local Methodist minister wrote to Chief Leonard about four of his young men who wished to visit police headquarters. They wanted to see the new communications center, and also to ride in a patrol car. He said the young men were trying to open a dialogue between the juveniles of their church and the police. The good Chief wrote that the demands of fighting crime did not permit the luxury of entertaining visitors except on the annual open house day of the police. The minister complained to a friend on the City Council and the City Manager was asked about it. He queried the Chief, "Why turn down a chance to improve police-community relations?" Chief Leonard told him: "If my budget request had been approved, maybe I could have done it—spared the time of one man—but there'll be no visits until I get more men." The City Manager asked the Chief to comply with the visit request. Chief Leonard thought it over, and stated his position loud and clear in a letter that he sent to the City Council, to the City Manager, and to the City Attorney for good measure. The letter was brief. It read: "The request by the City Manager to allow visitors to the police communications center and to ride in police patrol cars is an unlawful order issued arbitrarily and capriciously, and I have no intention of following out his order."

Now—the City Manager has called the press into his office. He has an important announcement to make.

CITY MANAGER: Gentlemen, I asked you to come over today to read to you a letter I've written to Police Chief Leonard. I shall pass around copies. Now I'll read it:

> Dear Chief Leonard:
> During the course of the past year, it has become evident that as police chief you have lost the confidence of the community, the members of the police department, and the city administration. Your actions and the conduct of your office have indicated that you do not understand or appreciate the duties and responsibilities of the position of police chief.
> Your actions and the conduct of your office have been severely criticized by the Human Rights Commission of our city, and by civic organizations that do not have any official connection with the city administration. They have called for your resignation.
> The Youth Bureau of our city, one of the most sensitive arms of the city government, especially in these troublesome times, has petitioned for your resignation. You do not have the necessary social awareness or attitude toward young people to carry out your job.
> Therefore under the power granted to the city manager in the city charter, I am dismissing you as police chief at the close of business, 5 P.M., today.

I hope you gentlemen will bear with me. This letter is the only item that will be released. It is self-explanatory, and I hope you will not press me for comment at this time.

NARRATOR: A few hours later, Chief Leonard called in the press, himself, and read them a letter he was sending to the state attorney general saying that he was about to be dismissed in an open-and-shut case of political retaliation; that a police captain and a city councilman were conspiring to have him replaced; and that he was asking the attorney general to investigate. He concluded his letter with this paragraph:

> I think it is a damned outrage that any police chief, not myself alone, can be summarily dismissed for professional police conduct of police operations without regard for outside political or partisan pressures.

QUESTIONS

1. Was City Manager Schmidt justified in firing Chief Leonard? (Justify your answer, either on the grounds that the termination was necessary for effective management, or that the dismissal was "political".)
2. Were Chief Leonard's actions to manage the department more effectively with the funds available a factor in his dismissal?

3. Was Chief Leonard's action in the Marquez transfer case justified, and could it properly be considered one of the incidents that necessitated his dismissal?

4. Can the attitudes of Chief Leonard, as exemplified by his response to corruption, "moonlighting," and the need for local police to collect "intelligence," be classified as desirable characteristics of a police executive?

5. Was Chief Leonard's rejection of the drug abuse group's request for a police speaker, and the clergyman's request to introduce young people from his church to police and police operations a legitimate contributory cause for his dismissal?

6. Was the apparent alienation of several groups of citizens a proper factor to consider in Chief Leonard's dismissal?

7. While morale is difficult to evaluate in any organization, do you believe that the dismissal of Chief Leonard might have adversely affected police morale?

The Struggle for Control of the New York City Police Department

During most of the last half of the nineteenth century, the control of the police force in New York City was really a "prize" awarded to the winner in New York's Mayoralty election. Election to this high municipal office usually required the support of New York City's dominant political party, the Democrats. By the 1890s, the time of this case study, New York City was famous for the "machine politics" of Tammany Hall, the organization of Democrats who had won power in city government time and again. Control of the police force was important to the Tammany politicians, because the "patronage" opportunities in the police force could be used to help a nominee win the Mayoralty election.[6]

This control of the operations of New York City's police was opposed by the dominant political party in state politics in New York. This was the Republican group which generally won gubernatorial elections because most of the state's rural areas and small cities voted for Republican nominees. It might be simply stated by saying that at the time of this case study the Republican nominees were voted into office by rich and well-to-do farmers and merchants living outside of New York City, and that the Democratic nominees of New York's Tammany Hall were elected by the businessmen and residents of New York City's heavily-populated low-rent areas.

In the course of government in New York City, a police officer named Thomas Byrnes became the top official of the New York Police Department; and a citizen identified with the Republican party, Theodore Roosevelt became President of New York City's "Police Commission."[7] Their

[6]Ralph G. Martin, *The Bosses* (New York: Putnam's, 1964), pp. 23–37.
[7]Stefan Lorant, *The Life and Times of Theodore Roosevelt* (Garden City, N.Y.: Doubleday, 1959), p. 269.

struggle for control of the New York Police Department spans a two-year period, dating from the 1894 revelations of the Rev. Charles H. Parkhurst, a noted municipal reformer, about corrupt dealings between the police and the city's underworld. While the case study is developed as a struggle between Byrnes and Roosevelt, the struggle between the political groups within the city at this time must also be appreciated to fully understand the situation.[8]

Thomas Byrnes was born in Ireland in 1842. He came to New York City as a child with the heavy tide of pre-Civil War Irish immigration. He grew up in the immigrant ghetto area, receiving some formal education and vocational training as a plumber and steam-fitter. He joined a New York volunteer regiment at the outbreak of the Civil War and served two years. In 1865 he applied for appointment to the New York City Police and was accepted. Three years later, in 1868, he was advanced to the rank of roundsman (field sergeant); and two years later, in 1870, to the rank of inspector. Inspector Byrnes' specialty was criminal investigation. He was made Chief of Detectives in 1880, while retaining the rank of inspector.

Byrnes was a big man, more than six feet tall and weighing over 200 pounds. He had an authoritative voice, shoulders, and posture. He believed the net worth of a detective was only measurable in results achieved. To achieve results, he learned the *modus operandi* of the professional criminal, developed a network of informers among the prostitutes and thieves of New York's underworld, and was one of the first criminal investigators to take advantage of the prisoner's dilemma: whether to remain silent or to confess before his crime partner or partners confessed. Inspector Byrnes said there was no honor among thieves, and that he had never met a criminal who would not talk if he could secure some concession from Byrnes for his cooperation.

There is little doubt that Byrnes was a stylist in criminal investigation. He looked for the telltale "signature" of the offender at crime scenes, used his network of informants to narrow the number of suspects, and then "picked them up" and questioned them. These operating procedures secured results. Later, as Chief of Detectives, he demanded the same thing from every detective: results.

It is alleged that Inspector Byrnes pursued criminals by establishing friendships in the underworld helpful in his work. On several occasions he recovered stolen property from thieves, burglars, and pickpockets within days of the report of the crime. No arrests were made in these cases, but it was demonstrated to the victim of the crime that Inspector Byrnes could produce results.

Byrnes established an innovative, though slightly unorthodox, police

[8]Wallace S. Sayre and Herbert Kaufman, *Governing New York City: Politics in the Metropolis* (New York: Russell Sage Foundation, 1960), pp. 289–90.

FIGURE 3 Inspector Thomas Byrnes, New York City Police Department.

procedure for deterring crime (or at least moving it elsewhere) when he initiated his "dead line" in 1880. Within the boundaries of a high-crime area in lower Manhattan, many jewelry shops—both wholesale and retail —were nestled along Maiden Lane, and only a few blocks away in Wall Street many banks operated in the neighborhood of the New York Stock Exchange. These businesses, their customers, and employees were the favorite victims of professional criminals. Byrnes outlined this area on a map, drawing a line from the East River at Fulton Street, west across Broadway to Greenwich Street, then south along Greenwich Street to the Battery— where the East River joined New York's Upper Bay. "You're dead if you go beyond this line," was his message to known thieves, burglars, forgers, counterfeiters, pickpockets, and confidence men. Byrnes put detectives on patrol in plainclothes in this area. These were experienced men who knew the faces of thousands of criminals. Known criminals who did violate the "dead line" were picked up and taken to jail and booked for one of their past crimes, or arrested under a special "vagrancy" ordinance in force at the time and applicable to known criminals.[9]

The "dead line" worked. Crime was reduced in this area of jewelry shops and banks. The business community praised Byrnes for his innova-

[9]James Richardson, *The New York Police: Colonial Times to 1901* (New York: Oxford University Press, 1970), pp. 209–13.

tive concept and no one questioned his actions on the legal grounds that these arrests were unconstitutional—mere presence in a high crime area being an unlikely substitute for the probable cause necessary to justify an arrest.

This *cordon sanitaire* appears to be characteristic of Byrnes and his relationships with criminals in New York City. Inspector Byrnes wrote in the *North American Review* in 1894 that before his "dead line" policy, New York City had been infested with criminals of all kinds. It was impossible to walk along the streets without rubbing up against them, he said, and respectable people were even being elbowed off the sidewalk by the criminals. In a comparatively short period of time since the "dead line" was initiated, Byrnes continued, every one of the criminals apprehended "below" the line was summoned to Police Headquarters, ordered to leave town, and to stay away. Byrnes had a defensive attitude about his contacts with criminals and his innovative crime-prevention technique. He concluded his articles by admitting that his measures may seem harsh and unjust, and that it may be thought to be cruel to arrest men on no specific charge and drive them from their place of residence, but he believed these men were professional criminals and that their presence in the city was a a menace to its safety.

In 1882 and 1883, at Inspector Byrnes's request, the Police Commission reorganized the Police Department's structure, placing all detectives under the direct command of the chief of detectives (many had been responsible to local police commanders). Greater efficiency was the rationale for the change, and it is true that centralization of the criminal investigative function is likely to lead to greater effectiveness in clearing cases by arrest or other means. But, the change also placed management of the entire city-wide criminal investigation function under the control of Tom Byrnes; and the decision as to what cases were to be assigned for active investigation would be made under his direction.

In 1888, a new post of Chief Inspector was created for Byrnes, so that he could function as chief of detectives and also serve as acting superintendent in the absence of the superintendent—the top rank in the police force of New York City. Finally, in 1892, Byrnes was appointed Superintendent of Police, the commander of the entire police force. In designating his successor as chief of detectives, Byrnes spoke of his own work with crime and criminals, saying that New York City now had a better criminal investigative unit than Scotland Yard, and that it was now without equal among the detective bureaus of the world.

Two years later, in 1894, a young clergyman embarked on a crusade to expose the corrupt relations between New York's underworld and the police. This crusader, the Reverend Charles H. Parkhurst of the Madison Square Presbyterian Church, excoriated Superintendent Byrnes, saying that Byrnes should know of this unholy relationship between thieves and police because of his years as a detective, and that he was an incompetent if he did not know of it, and a malignant presence in his executive police position if he did not correct it, or at least cooperate in cleaning it up!

Parkhurst went into the high crime areas to collect his own evidence, and he then made it public. His work led to an investigation by a state crime commission chaired by an "upstate" Senator named Clarence Lexow. It was an inquiry in depth and, regardless of its political overtones, the report of the Lexow Committee, in December 1894, shocked the people of New York. It traced police "protection" to gamblers and prostitutes who paid various sums each month to a police officer termed the "bag man," who then distributed the money among his police associates. Bribery was extensive and appeared to involve the police commanders in the field, as well as their subordinates.

In the public reaction to Parkhurst's disclosures, a reform mayor was elected at the next general election. William L. Strong, the new mayor, was elected on a non-partisan "fusion" ticket. Now the city had a mayor who had no obligation to either of the major political parties, the Republicans or the Democrats. The Good Government Club, which had supported the work of Reverend Parkhurst, had a pledge from the new mayor that his administration would be nonpartisan and would strive for police reform. Strong acted promptly, and appointed Theodore Roosevelt as President of the four-man Police Commission.

This commission existed because of an earlier agreement between state and municipal officials. Its membership was to be equally representative of both major political parties: two registered Democrats and two registered Republicans. The role of this commission was to give bipartisan leadership to the police force of New York City.

Theodore Roosevelt was a man of wealth, education, and social position. He was honest, sincere, and energetic, and was involved in politics and an activist in seeking good government.[10] He did not view his appointment as a political assignment, or his job as simply that of another member of the police commission. He saw himself and his role as that of chief peace officer of the City of New York. In later years, after service as assistant secretary of the Navy and as president of the United States, Roosevelt indicated this attitude in his autobiography. He wrote that he was appointed by Mayor Strong with the distinct understanding that he was to administer the Police Department with entire disregard of partisan politics, and only from the viewpoint of a good citizen interested in promoting the welfare of the community and its citizens.[11]

Two minor incidents are illustrative of the zest of the new "Chief

[10]Theodore Roosevelt, *An Autobiography* (New York: Macmillan, 1919), pp. 185–88.
[11]William Roscoe Thayer, *Theodore Roosevelt: An Intimate Biography* (Boston: Houghton Mifflin, 1919) pp. 98–105.

FIGURE 4 **Theodore Roosevelt, Chairman of the New York City Board of Police Commissioners in 1894 and 1895. Roosevelt ousted Inspector Thomas Byrnes as Superintendent of Police. Appointed by a "reform" mayor, Roosevelt believed Byrnes was unable or unwilling to cooperate with him in Roosevelt's plan to reorganize New York City's police department.**

Peace Officer" and his orientation toward his new work. Mayor Strong had first offered Roosevelt the position of commissioner of the street cleaning department. He refused the appointment, saying it was not in his line, although he would have been delighted to smash up the corrupt contractors and put the street-cleaning force absolutely out of the domain of politics. Later, in accepting the police position, Roosevelt said the work of police was in his line and he was glad to undertake it.

Roosevelt viewed his new position as requiring the dual task of both actually handling the Police Department as its manager and of using this management to help in making the city a better place in which to live and work for persons in the middle and lower socio-economic levels of the community. At the time, he expressed his hope that Mr. Strong would be a workingman's mayor rather than a businessman's mayor.

Roosevelt publicly stated, at this time, that the existing rules for the governance of the police made it difficult to accomplish anything worthwhile, and that the checks and balances established by law to control the executive power of the police commissioners were ideally suited to encourage intrigue, conspiracy, and politics. He noted that these rules for administering the Police Department had been planned so that no man would have power enough to do anything bad but, as it turned out, the rules prevented anyone from doing good, also.

Roosevelt's fight to keep politics and every kind of improper favoritism out of his management of the police department led to his summary dismissal of Thomas Byrnes as Superintendent. As a Republican in good standing, Roosevelt was close to Senator Lexow and the work of his committee, and as a personal friend and supporter of the Reverend Parkhurst and his crusade, he was familiar with the truth of the thief-police alliance. From both sources, Roosevelt received support for his opinion that the removal of Byrnes was vital to improving the police.

Byrnes fought the good fight, as Roosevelt might have termed it, by denying the findings of both Parkhurst and the Lexow Committee. He claimed Parkhurst was an "amateur" investigator misled by underworld informants, and that the Lexow Committee was "pure politics." Byrnes's pinpointing of Republican party leaders as dictating the findings of the Lexow Committee was not without evidence and his claim was accepted by many leaders in New York City's business community. Probably, Byrnes's past record of fighting criminals who preyed on business and commerce in the city was a real asset in his fight to disclaim the charges by Parkhurst and the findings of the Lexow Committee.

However, the new police commissioner's enthusiasm and sincerity was apparent to the general public, and Roosevelt was able to win over a few hostile segments of the community by personal appearances and speeches about his intention to improve the police. He might not have succeeded in eventually dismissing Byrnes if it were not for his own fight for community understanding, and for the fact that New York City was in one of its periodic lapses into virtue.

Byrnes managed to have a bill introduced in the State Legislature which would transfer the existing power of the police commission of New York City and its commissioners to a new office of "Chief," who would be selected from the ranks of the uniformed force, thus excluding Roosevelt from any consideration for the post, and because of his own preeminence in the City's force, it practically assured Byrnes of the appointment for himself. It was shrewd in-fighting, but Roosevelt fought back. On May 10, 1895, he wrote Governor Charles T. Saxon, a fellow anti-machine Republican who was interested in reform government, that the proposed legislation was vicious and obviously designed to perpetuate the worst and most corrupt practices which had flourished in the Police Department. He noted that it would reduce the Police Commission to a nullity and place the power of management of the police in the hands of the new "Chief." He asked the Governor to alert their mutual friends in the state legislature to the bill's true character, and to point out that the passage of this proposed legislation would be an act of scandalous iniquity. He concluded his letter with an appeal: "I write to you because I know I can always appeal to you on grounds of decent citizenship and of a sincere desire to benefit the Republican party."[12]

[12]Eltinge E. Morison, *The Letters of Theodore Roosevelt*, vol. 1 (Cambridge: Harvard University Press, 1951), p. 455.

At the same time, Roosevelt was busy attempting to push his own legislation for reorganizing the Police Department through the state legislature. He sought the power to remove undesirable subordinates without appeal to the courts, and he pleaded that this power was vital to any thorough and radical reform of the police establishment. Without it, he said that he could still improve matters a good deal, but that he could not do what he ought to.

The state senate and assembly approved Roosevelt's "Police Reorganization Bill" for the New York City Police Department. In this legislation, the police commission (chaired by Roosevelt at the time) was given the power to appoint and remove the superintendent of police, the chief inspector, the chief of detectives, and all officers above the rank of captain. The legislation specified that removal had to be for cause, but it did not establish any appeal from the decision of the police commission.

In a letter to a friend in Albany, the state capitol, Roosevelt discussed removing Byrnes, now that the power of removal was in the hands of the police commission. He asked his friend to sound out a prominent Republican political leader, Elihu Root, whom he believed to be a supporter of Byrnes. Characteristically, Roosevelt wrote that even if Root backed up Byrnes it "will make no difference in my action, except that I wish to be prepared in advance."[13]

On the following day, in a letter to Henry Cabot Lodge, a close friend and an associate active in Republican national politics, Roosevelt did not mince any words. He wrote:

> I think I shall move against Byrnes at once. I thoroughly distrust him, and cannot do any thorough work while he remains. It will be a very hard fight, and I have no idea how it will come out.[14]

Within a month of receiving extended powers under the 1895 Police Reorganization Bill, the police commission discussed a recommendation by Roosevelt that the employment of Thomas Byrnes as superintendent of the New York City Police Department be terminated for cause. Roosevelt cited Byrnes's general record of failing to cooperate with the police commission in its attempt to stamp out the police-underworld alliance and his specific unwillingness to appoint an honest police commander in New York City's "Tenderloin"—an area described by the Reverend Parkhurst to the Lexow Committee as the center of crime operations and police "protection" to criminals. The vote for removal was unanimous, as was the commission's action on a subsequent motion by Roosevelt to remove Byrnes's appointee as police commander of the "Tenderloin," Inspector Alexander S. Williams. The record noted Williams was terminated "for good and sufficient reasons."

[13]Morison, *Letters*, pp. 456–57.
[14]Ibid., pp. 457–58.

An epilogue to this struggle for control of the New York City Police Department is contained in a single sentence from a letter dated June 2, 1895, and which Roosevelt sent to his sister Anna. The sentence reads: "I am getting the Police Department under control; I forced Byrnes and Williams out, and now hold undisputed sway."[15]

QUESTIONS

1. Was the Police Commission action in terminating the employment of Byrnes as Police Superintendent justified?
2. Was the "dead line" established by Byrnes a proper method of controlling crime?
3. Was the proven existence of "protection" payments to police by gamblers and prostitutes to gain immunity from arrest legitimate grounds for the dismissal of Byrnes?
4. Was the assumption of the role of "chief peace officer" by Roosevelt an example of review of police practice by a "police review board," or was it community control of police behavior?

SUMMARY

The three case studies in this chapter are illustrative of an unresolved problem in government: how should a community judge police behavior? These cases also stress the question of where the ultimate decision about the conduct of a police leader should be made. In the first two cases, it was made at the municipal level; in the Byrnes-Roosevelt struggle for control of the police force in New York City, it was made at the state level of government. While each case presents the basic question of whether the dismissal of the police executive was justified by the sparse facts of the case study, a collateral question of equal or greater importance is whether the procedures for these terminations are valid, reliable, and in the best interests of the police and the community.

[15]Anna Roosevelt Cowles, *Letters from Theodore Roosevelt: 1870–1918* (New York: Scribner's, 1924), pp. 154–56.

CHAPTER TWO

Judicial Review and Police Standards

In the beginning there were magistrates. There were justices of the peace in the Anglo-American history of criminal justice before there were police. As examining magistrates, these justices of the peace acted out the roles of both police and prosecutor, as well as acting in their judicial roles. Aggrieved citizens brought complaints to court for action when a crime was known or suspected.

Anglo-American law still hews to the line that the primary responsibility for determining whether a person shall be taken into custody, and whether he shall be held for a formal accusatory proceeding and trial, should be vested in the judiciary. This is the concept that the judiciary should review police investigation and action on its merits in each individual case, either prior to the police action—in an application before a magistrate for a search or arrest warrant; or after a warrantless arrest, or search and seizure—in a hearing before a magistrate to justify the summary police action.

For many years, judicial action to secure fundamental fairness for persons accused of crime was confined to the trial and the post-trial period. More recently, judicial emphasis has been on the pretrial period. There has been an emerging judicial belief that the opportunity of an accused person to have a fair trial can be short-circuited in the period prior to trial by various police and prosecution practices which would tend to grossly prejudice any subsequent trial.

Any free society is confronted with the problem of establishing a basic liberty for citizens in the community, in the face of the government's use of its monopoly of force. In the United States, the Constitution and its Bill of Rights established a reasonable balance between the conflicting claims of public order and safety, and the liberty and rights of individual citizens. After the Civil War, amendments to the Constitution expanded the constitutional protection of individual liberty. The Fourteenth Amendment contained clauses forbidding states and state agents from denying due process of law, equal protection of the laws, and the privileges and immunities of federal citizenship.

These constitutional strictures, and laws that have derived from them, have governed much of the operations of law enforcement agents. Law enforcement agents are assigned a role in which they must balance the personal liberty of an individual against the attacks on public safety and order by criminals.

Judicial review of law enforcement and its agents has developed a body of case law which defines the rights of all parties involved, and outlines acceptable police procedures by defining the limitations and responsibilities of the police. The cases in this chapter are illustrative of some of the standards of police behavior established by the United States Supreme Court in its decisions which define the ordinary citizen's right to be let alone and to enjoy the due process of law when confronted by police and accused of crime.

Case Study 4, the first case in this chapter, is concerned with the reasonableness of police search and seizure of evidence. The landmark case in this area is *Mapp v. Ohio.*[1] This decision of the U.S. Supreme Court reaffirmed the Court's earlier decision to exclude evidence at criminal trials which was illegally obtained by police. In earlier decisions,[2] the Court had set standards of reasonableness in search and seizures for federal agents and courts; in *Mapp*, the Court utilized the Fourteenth Amendment's guarantee of "due process" to set the same standards for state agents and courts.

Case Study 5 is concerned with the individual citizen's right to be let alone—as opposed to the police power to stop and question persons. This case study is based on the facts of an Ohio case, *Terry v. Ohio.*[3] The merit of the police action in this case was based on the steadily-increasing police practice of field interrogation.[4] The merits of the defense case rested on the constitutional protection of privacy, as affirmed in *Mapp v. Ohio.*[5] The U.S. Supreme Court agreed to review the Ohio trial court's conviction of Terry. It is believed that the Court's acceptance of this case was based on two facts: (1) a serious concern over the prevailing practices in police field interrogations, and (2) failure of the Court to review such cases in the past and to establish guidelines for this relatively new police practice.

Terry's appeal failed. The court held that the police officer in this case had acted properly in stopping Terry and conducting a limited search

[1]367 U.S. 643 (1961).

[2]*Weeks v. U.S.*, 232 U.S. 383 (1914) *Elkins v. U.S.*, 364 U.S. 206 (1960).

[3]392 U.S. 1 (1967).

[4]Lawrence Tiffany, Donald M. McIntyre, Jr., and Daniel L. Rotenberg, *Detection of Crime* (Boston: Little Brown, 1967), pp. 87–94.

[5]367 U.S. 643 (1961).

of Terry's outer clothing in an attempt to discover weapons which might be used against the officer; that such a search is a reasonable one under the Fourth Amendment; and that any weapons seized may properly be introduced in evidence against the person from whom they were taken. The factual data of the Terry case has been expanded and dramatized to present the situation for student analysis and evaluation. (This case is not presented for a legal analysis of the Court's decision or the content of the majority opinion in this case.)

The last case in this chapter, Case Study 6, reviews a police attempt at interrogating a non-cooperative and silent suspect. The case has been included in order to highlight the police interrogation practices which have been detailed in police textbooks, and were later severely criticized by the U.S. Supreme Court, in *Miranda v. Arizona*.[6] The Court claimed that these practices jeopardize a suspect's Fifth Amendment privileges against self-incrimination.

In total, these three cases illustrate decisional law which now governs police practices of search and seizure, stop and frisk, and custodial interrogation.[7]

[6]384 U.S. 436 (1966).

[7]A term resulting from the U.S. Supreme Court's decision in *Escobedo v. Illinois*, 378 U.S. 478 (1964), and *Miranda v. Arizona*, 384 U.S. 436 (1966). It identifies a point in a criminal investigation when a case is focused on a suspect, he is taken into police custody or otherwise deprived of his freedom, and questioned by police.

The "Pot" Party

This case study has three major characters and three scenes. It begins with the arraignment of an arrested person before a magistrate on the signed "complaint" of the arresting officer which states that he had probable cause to arrest the defendant, and cites the criminal charges placed against the accused person. It ends with the defendant walking out of court, a free man.

CAST OF CHARACTERS

Judge ANONYMOUS
Police Officer JOHN MULDOON
Defendant RON MCBLADE

SCENE 1: *A prisoner is being arraigned. He stands alongside a man with a police badge hanging from his coat lapel. Both men are facing the Judge's bench. The time is a day after the prisoner was arrested.*

JUDGE: You have a right to counsel at every stage of these proceedings against you, and you and your counsel will be given a written copy of this complaint—of these charges against you. Do you have funds for legal counsel?

DEFENDANT: Your Honor, I am a member of the bar, I will act as my own attorney.

JUDGE: I thought I recognized you—

DEFENDANT: I'm ashamed of my appearance, your Honor and I must apologize to the court, but— The police would not permit me, would not—

JUDGE: That's perfectly all right. Do you want a continuance at this time?

DEFENDANT: No, I would like to get on with it. I am anxious to vindicate myself. I am more than ready— This is a case of guilt by association.

JUDGE: (*Interrupting*) Tell us about this arrest, officer.

OFFICER MULDOON: We had information from a reliable informant, your Honor, that a certain group of drug users were going to hold a marijuana party—a pot party. The location given us was apartment number 4 at 6000 River Road. We checked out the tenant, a man named Jones, and found him to be a known drug user with two or three convictions. He is on probation, in fact. We went to court, to Justice Walsh, and got a search warrant. We went to that apartment, kept it under observation, and about an hour after the party got under way—we went in. We got a wagonload of people and pot, and some indecent articles. All told, we made 13 arrests.

JUDGE: Was this defendant in the apartment when you entered under the authority of the search warrant?

OFFICER MULDOON: No— Most of them, including the tenant, were in there when we hit the place; but this one, the defendant (*nodding to McBlade*), was a late arrival.

JUDGE: He came to the party alone, after you had entered?

OFFICER MULDOON: That's right. We were just about ready to leave when he rang the bell. (*Firmly*) Now, we knew that no one was coming to that place just by chance that night, and that he was there for the party. So we searched him as soon as he stepped into the room. He was in a place where marijuana was being smoked.

DEFENDANT: Your Honor, could I have that corrected? There was no marijuana being smoked at that time. Most of the people I saw were handcuffed, and the others appeared to be with him (*indicating Muldoon*).

JUDGE: Officer, what are the facts on this point?

OFFICER MULDOON: (*Reflectively*) Well— Just as I said, we were about ready to go— But he didn't come there to see us. He came to the party—

JUDGE: (*Interrupting*) Then, the defendant was not in the place at the time that marijuana was being smoked?

OFFICER MULDOON: Yes and no. Technically, no. All right— No! But we found plenty of pot in his apartment.

DEFENDANT: Your Honor, I want to raise a timely objection to the search of my home; it was completely without legal justification.

OFFICER MULDOON: It was all legal, buddy (*to McBlade*)—and (*to Judge*) we went to court, Justice Walsh, and got a search warrant. It was all legal!

JUDGE: I see from these attachments to the complaint that a search warrant was procured, but (*reading*) I note that the probable cause given to Justice Walsh was that marijuana had been found on the defendant in a search incidental to his arrest. Is this true?

OFFICER MULDOON: Yes. We found shreds and a couple of seeds in his right coat pocket when we put him against the wall at the apartment.

DEFENDANT: Your Honor, I don't want to dispute at this time whether the substance allegedly found was, in fact, marijuana; but I do want to raise the issue that whatever was found was the fruit of an illegal search, incidental to an illegal arrest.

JUDGE: When an arrest is not justified, is the resultant search equally unjustified?

DEFENDANT: Yes, your Honor. I know, with your experience on the bench and knowledge of the law, that I don't have to cite cases—

JUDGE: I'll take judicial notice of my extensive experience. Did you (*to Muldoon*) have any information concerning this defendant before you entered this apartment for the purpose of executing the search warrant? Just answer yes or no.

OFFICER MULDOON: (*Grumbling*) No— But that is— Not by name— No.

JUDGE: Was there anything about the appearance of this defendant at the time, just prior to making this arrest, or any of his conduct at this time, that would—in any way—suggest he was "high," "on drugs," or had drugs in his possession?

OFFICER MULDOON: No, he looked like any of the others, like an ordinary guy—but he did appear where a pot party was going to be held, and was held.

JUDGE: Please answer yes or no.

OFFICER MULDOON: You know that's a "no" answer.

JUDGE: (*to Muldoon*) Courts have held that mere presence at the scene of a crime, even coupled with a prior criminal conviction—and we do not have that in this case—is not probable cause for an arrest. Now—from your expertise as a police officer, Mr. Muldoon—have you now, or did you have at the time of this arrest, any inference that the defendant was in some way involved in the commission of the crime of unlawful possession of drugs in relation to these 12 other persons arrested?

OFFICER MULDOON: "No" to that. He rang the bell; we arrested him; we frisked him; found the shreds and seeds in his pocket; got a search warrant; found more stuff in his apartment (*offering package*); and that's it!

JUDGE: (*Kindly*) A very good summation.

DEFENDANT: If the Court pleases, the crime committed in the apartment was the possession of drugs forbidden by law. This type of crime is such that by its very nature it is unique to the individual in possession, and possibly those in his company—but not *ex post facto*. The possessor is the criminal in this type of crime.

JUDGE: Other than the possessor, then it is guilt by association? An interesting concept.

OFFICER MULDOON: We got the possessor, the tenant, and we charged him with possession. We charged the others with "being in a place—"

JUDGE: I have it right here, officer. Thank you. (*Reading*) Then you have no probable cause to connect this defendant with the possession of drugs found on any other person. Is that correct?

OFFICER MULDOON: That's correct.

JUDGE: Officer, did you, at the time this defendant entered the apartment, have any reason to infer that he was armed and dangerous and that your own safety or that of one or more of your associates was in danger?

OFFICER MULDOON: No. These pot-heads don't worry me. No, not this class of user. No, I didn't frisk him for guns or a knife.

JUDGE: Officer, you have failed to establish probable cause for the arrest of this defendant, and I therefore discharge him. The evidence you have proffered was the fruit of an illegal search—since the arrest itself was illegal—and it is therefore excluded. It is not admissible evidence against the defendant under these circumstances. However, since it is contraband, I order that it be properly disposed of in accordance with the law. Case dismissed.

Good morning to you, counselor. And officer—I suggest that you carry back to your associates the message of this transaction here in this court today.

QUESTIONS

1. On the facts of this case, was the judge's action justified?
2. Was the fact that the evidence had been seized under the authority of a search warrant a factor in the decision in this case?
3. Was the time factor in relation to the arrival of the defendant at the

place of arrest, and the planned departure by police with their prisoners, a factor of importance in this case?

4. Is it likely that the attitude of the police witness (Officer Muldoon) was a factor in the court's decision?

5. Did the judicial admonition to the police witness (and his associates), at the close of this hearing, indicate bias and prejudice?

The Terry Case

This case study has a cast of characters common to proceedings in criminal courts in America. The dialogue of the single scene of this case study is a simplification of the usual court transcript and the formalities of an original arraignment, or preliminary examination, before a magistrate. It is a style that rejects the classic "question and answer" form of court transcripts for a form that "moves the story."

CAST OF CHARACTERS

Judge (Magistrate)	ANONYMOUS
Suspect	JOHN TERRY
Associate of Suspect	RICHARD CHILTON
Associate of Suspect	CHARLES KATZ
Defense Attorney	ANONYMOUS
Arresting Officer	DETECTIVE THOMAS ("MAC") MACFADDEN

SCENE 1: *Courtroom of local magistrate. The trio speaking stand in front of the judge's bench. MacFadden is at Terry's right, while the defense attorney is at Terry's left.*

JUDGE (*To arrestee Terry and attorney*): Now that we have dispensed with the preliminaries and the reading of the complaint, let's talk about this— I don't like to say summary arrest—but I will say "stop-and-frisk," that resulted in an arrest. Officer MacFadden, why did you stop these defendants in the first instance?

OFFICER MACFADDEN: They were doing something funny. It looked funny to me, odd that is—like they were "casing a job," to do a stickup —an armed robbery.

TERRY: We hadn't *done* anything.

ATTORNEY: My client and his friend, Mr. Richard Chilton, have certain rights to free assembly—to move about without being molested by the the police.

OFFICER MACFADDEN: I'm thirty-nine years a policeman next March; thirty-five years of them I've been a detective; and for thirty years I've been assigned to downtown Cleveland—working boosters and dips; shoplifters and pickpockets. In this case, when I first saw these men, they didn't look right to me.

TERRY: We were just thinking about something. We didn't *do* anything.

ATTORNEY: A lot of people may not look "right"; but is that any cause, any probable cause, to stop them and search them? Probable cause only exists when the officer's information is reasonable and sufficient, standing alone, to warrant a reasonable and cautious man to believe an offense has been, or is being committed.

JUDGE: True; but let's hear more—

OFFICER MACFADDEN: I watched the two of them, and their movements. First, one of them, Terry that is, would walk from the corner—that's Huron Road and Euclid Avenue—down the row of stores. He just sauntered along, casual-like, but he kept giving one store a real look-over. Then the other, Chilton, that's his name, would talk to his partner, Terry, for a moment. Then, *he* would mosey down the row of stores, and would give this same store a real look-over, go past it, turn around, come back and talk to his partner on the corner.

TERRY: We didn't really *do* anything.

ATTORNEY: A lot of people walk and talk, and do window shopping. There is nothing criminal in this type of conduct.

OFFICER MACFADDEN: I either stand and watch people, or I walk and watch people. That's what I've been doing for years. I thought these two were worth a little attention when I first saw them together, and then I saw them together, again, a few minutes later, though they had just separated a few moments before. One, that is, going off by himself. I got more purpose to watch them when I seen these movements—back and forth—repeated.

TERRY: There was a lot of people on the street. Not just us.

OFFICER MACFADDEN: Yes, and one of them stopped and talked to these two. I found out later his name was Katz.

ATTORNEY: Yes, when my client was arrested and charged by Detective

MacFadden, Mr. Charles Katz—who was also "brought in"—had to be released.

TERRY: Yes, Katz came up and talked with Chilton and me—but that's not a crime.

OFFICER MACFADDEN: It was almost like they were walking a foot post, back and forth, always looking into this one store. They made five or six trips altogether, each of them, more than a dozen trips in all, over a period of about ten minutes. I followed them when they finally walked off—down Euclid Avenue.

ATTORNEY: How can police find time to follow people who have not indicated any criminal intent by an overt act?

OFFICER MACFADDEN: Let me finish— I might have kept following them or even forgot about the whole thing, but then I saw them meet this third man again, this Katz, and then I jumped them.

TERRY: Man, just meeting another guy and this cop puts the law on us—

ATTORNEY: People have a right to be let alone—unless and until the officer has probable cause to make an arrest, and it is a constitutional right—a basic and valid right.

OFFICER MACFADDEN: Maybe so, but not when they're carrying guns. I thought they would have guns and when I stopped them I was careful. "Get the gun first," I thought. I grabbed Terry, and I put him between me and the other two—Chilton and Katz. I patted him down fast and found it, the gun, under his overcoat. A good feel, I knew it was a gun, and he knew it too, so did the others. My first thought was three to one —bad odds.

ATTORNEY: A policeman might search many passers-by and find guns; but the law does not give police that right.

TERRY: I knew he realized it was a gun. Hell, a gun feels like a gun—it don't feel like nothing else.

OFFICER MACFADDEN: We were in front of Zuker's store. I've known Zuker for years. I kept Terry close to me, and told all three of them: "Into the store, get into the store." As we went in, I shucked the overcoat off of Terry. The gun was in the inside left breast pocket and I was afraid to get tangled up with him in getting it out. I wouldn't have been able to watch the other two. Now, I had the coat and a gun, and I saw Zuker in back of the store coming around his back counter. I called to him.

ATTORNEY: Any search, any seizure at this time was completely unconstitutional. My client had not attempted a crime or given the officer probable cause to arrest.

TERRY: He made us stand against the store wall with our hands up. You know, up against the wall, with your hands over your head.

OFFICER MACFADDEN: Yes. I lined the three of them up. I frisked Katz, and then this Chilton. When I felt the gun in Chilton's overcoat pocket, I told him to freeze, and then I lifted it out. Now I had two guns, three people—and I heard Zuker saying: "I already put in the call for the cars—they'll be right here."

ATTORNEY: Who knows how many people, of all the pedestrians on any street in downtown Cleveland, may be carrying weapons. True, carrying weapons, under some circumstances, may be against the law; but it is also against the law to interfere with a citizen's right to walk the streets in peace and tranquility.

TERRY: We hadn't *done* anything. We hadn't used the guns. We hadn't even gone into a store. We never left the sidewalk until we got ordered into a store—after the cop took my overcoat.

OFFICER MACFADDEN: The two that had the guns were given a good search at police headquarters. We brought the three of them in, but we let Katz go after we had a good identification on him. I charged both Terry and Chilton with illegal possession of concealed firearms, a violation of Ohio law, and put the two guns—and the cartridges that I also found—in the evidence locker.

ATTORNEY: Yes, and under Ohio law it may be possible to convict my client; but it will be a miscarriage of justice.

TERRY: We don't deny the policeman found the guns. But, everyone said he didn't have any real right to give us that "Hey you" routine, and stop and frisk us.

OFFICER MACFADDEN: First, they didn't look right to me. Then I took up a position in a doorway about 400 feet away and watched them. To me, they were "casing a job"—probably a robbery.

ATTORNEY: Suspicion alone is *not* probable cause—

OFFICER MACFADDEN: They didn't look right to me. I had a duty to stop them. That's what I'm paid to do in downtown Cleveland. I had a right to protect myself, and that's all I did. Say that I gave them a "protective" search—protective for me, that is.

ATTORNEY: That's the sad part of this case. Police cannot stop people and search them without probable cause. There are limitations on stops and searches.

OFFICER MACFADDEN: If I hadn't stopped them and frisked them, what might Terry and his friend Chilton, and their friend Katz, have done later that day with those two guns?

TERRY: I'd rather be caught really *doing* something—

JUDGE: An interesting legality here: the police stop, and the superficial search is justified by the arresting officer's story. He tells us of his objective reasoning based on the observation of a man skilled in the methods of criminals, and on this basis he believed it his duty as a police officer to stop and question the defendant and his associates. The search was incidental to his initial action. It was not an unreasonable intrusion. Under the circumstances, the officer believed these men might be armed and he limited his search procedure to determining whether they were armed. Then, finding the guns, the officer proceeded as provided by the law of this state. I believe there is probable cause for summary arrest without a warrant on the charge specified in this complaint. The defendant is held to answer. The case is referred to the prosecutor. At this time I will review the defense request to set bail for the defendant.

QUESTIONS

1. Do the facts and testimony in this case study warrant the judicial decision to hold the defendant to answer to the charges of illegally possessing a dangerous weapon?

2. Was Detective MacFadden's years of experience, and resultant expertise in the methods of criminals, a factor in the court's decision?

3. What are the basic facts which support the judicial conclusion that Detective MacFadden had developed probable cause for this arrest by reasoning objectively from his observations of Terry and his associates?

4. Was Detective MacFadden's statements, about his fear that Terry and his associates might be armed, justified?

5. Is it within the scope of judicial review to decide if it is necessary for police to search persons for weapons when they are stopped under circumstances such as those in this case?

Joe Sigal–the Silent Suspect

The most uncooperative suspect is the one who will not talk at all, or who is reluctant to discuss his possible involvement in the crime in which he is a major suspect. This case study presents the struggle between the detectives who are certain of a suspect's guilt as a result of their investigation and collection of evidence, and a suspect who is unwilling to admit his guilt—either because of his innocence, or his belief that this is not the time to admit his guilt. The case study is presented in three scenes. At the time of the first scene the defendant is in custody and is being fingerprinted by Detective #1, Thomas Clancy. In the second scene Detective Clancy and Detective #2, Charles Weber, function as a "team" in interrogating Sigal. In the last scene, the Assistant Prosecutor assigned to the case attempts to secure a confession, or some admissions, from Sigal. In total, the three scenes depict the "pressure" of police interrogation. This "pressure," and its likely effect on the person being interrogated, was the subject of extensive comment in the U.S. Supreme Court's majority opinion in *Miranda v. Arizona*.[8]

CAST OF CHARACTERS

1st Detective	THOMAS CLANCY
2nd Detective	CHARLES WEBER
Assistant Prosecutor	ANTHONY PUGLESE
Suspect	JOE SIGAL

[8]384 U.S. 436 (1966).

SCENE 1: *Police station, detective office; Joe Sigal is being fingerprinted by detective Clancy. Sigal is in police custody, under arrest.*

DETECTIVE CLANCY: How do you spell it?

SUSPECT: J-O-E.

DETECTIVE CLANCY: No, dum-dum, Sigal.

SUSPECT: S-I-G-A-L.

DETECTIVE CLANCY: Okay (*writing, then starting to fingerprint suspect*). Look, I'm only saying this because it's just the facts. Sometimes people do things in a fit of anger, in temper, but they aren't really responsible for what they did. It's the temper, the anger, the rage— See what I mean. It's murder; but it isn't quite murder— See—

SUSPECT: No, I don't see it. All I know is that I didn't do it. You got the wrong guy.

DETECTIVE CLANCY: (*Continuing with the fingerprinting*) Okay, okay. It's just that a man provoked, a man in anger or temper has some excuse, some justification. Something you can tell your lawyer: "Look, I did it, but the S.O.B. brought it on himself."

SUSPECT: You mean that if he got me angry, and I— No. No. You got the wrong guy— You mean there's an "out" if there's a pro—

DETECTIVE CLANCY: Provocation. Yes, provocation. He got you burned up. He made you go after him, to be a man, to prove it. You probably didn't go out looking for trouble. My guess is, however, that you expected something from him and that's why you carried a gun—for your own protection. You knew him for what he was—no good. Then when you met him, he probably started using foul, abusive language, and he gave some indication that he was about to pull a gun on you—and that's when you had to act to save your own life. That's about it, isn't it, Joe?

SUSPECT: (*Slowly*) I think I better talk to my lawyer first. I don't trust you. You got a job to do. It's not— (*hastily*) I don't think you're a good guy, this is your job. Me— I'm the only guy who's for me. I only trust me—or maybe my lawyer—

DETECTIVE CLANCY: I give you an "out" for a murder, self-defense, and you don't buy it. I don't understand you.

SUSPECT: (*Bewildered*) Self-defense— What— I don't get the drift. All I know is that we shouldn't be talking. You're trying to get me to say something I shouldn't. I mean, I don't want to say anything. I shouldn't be talking at all.

DETECTIVE CLANCY: Why not? If the guy acted so that he provoked you —or you thought he did—that's a good defense. Morally, that's moral justification. I might do the same thing myself. Who would blame you?

SUSPECT: I don't know. All I know is that I should talk to someone, other than you—a friend, a lawyer. That's what I need, a lawyer.

DETECTIVE CLANCY: I'm your friend, I want to help you, but we don't have all day. Let's get this over with. You ready to tell the truth.

SUSPECT: What have I got to tell. I've been telling you the truth for a long time now.

DETECTIVE CLANCY: Don't give me that jazz. If you had been telling the truth, do you think I'd still be here with you? What have I got in common with you? You're a burglar. I'm a policeman. Let's cut the clowning—I'm sick and tired of it. I've a good mind—

SCENE 2: *Police station, interrogation room, no windows, no pictures on wall. Joe Sigal and Detective Clancy have been joined by Detective Weber. The three men are seated around a large table. The time is shortly after the fingerprinting in Scene 1.*

DETECTIVE WEBER: Cool off, Clancy. Cool it, man. You're being—you're off the beam—

DETECTIVE CLANCY: What's with you? You're supposed to be my partner. I'm beginning to think you're his partner—You're some help! (*Gets up from chair, moves to door, and exits.*)

DETECTIVE WEBER: He doesn't mean it. He's a guy who upsets easy. He's not a bad guy. But now he's going over to the boss to beef about us, about me— I shouldn't have butted in. The boss doesn't like it. There's a lot of headaches in this job.

SUSPECT: Boy, he sure has a temper. I didn't mean to get him all riled up. What did I do?

DETECTIVE WEBER: It's what you didn't do. He's sure he built up a good case. He knows he can convict you. He just wants you to tell him.

SUSPECT: Cripes! This is my second felony. If I cop out on this one I go away for a long time. I just can't—

DETECTIVE WEBER: (*Interrupting*) You can't afford not to. He gets awful mad. He's coming back. Don't forget that! Maybe he's got the boss to take me off the case. If he's mad, he's not in a mood to help you— Maybe, while I'm still on the case— Look, we get along— Tell me a little bit, and when he comes back, I'll tell him. Let me handle it. Give up a little bit, and I can go to the boss and fight to stay on the case myself, and dump Clancy. That way you're working with a friend—

SUSPECT: I dunno— You guys work together. Don't con me. When do I get a lawyer?

SCENE 3: *Same as Scene 2, the police interrogation room. Anthony Puglese, the assigned Assistant Prosecutor, sits opposite Sigal.*

TIME: *About three hours after previous scene.*

ASSISTANT PROSECUTOR PUGLESE: I'm not here to force you to talk. You have a right to remain silent. That's your privilege and I'm the last person who'll try to take it away from you. If that's the way you want it, okay. But— Let me ask you this: Suppose you were in my shoes, and I were in yours, and you called me in to ask me about this and I told you, "I don't want to answer any of your questions." You'd probably be right in thinking that I had something to hide. That's exactly what I'll have to think about you, and so will everybody else. So let's sit here and talk about it—talk the whole thing over.

SUSPECT: I just don't feel I should talk about it. I don't know anything.

ASSISTANT PROSECUTOR PUGLESE: It's to your advantage to tell the truth. If you did get involved in this—this trouble—the truth will get you out of here. If you did it, it's better to get it off your chest.

SUSPECT: It's your business to send people to jail. You're not sending me away.

ASSISTANT PROSECUTOR PUGLESE: I'm not trying to send you to prison. I just want you to level with me, to tell the truth. Your mother, your father, your lawyer—eh—wouldn't they all want you to tell the truth? Haven't you been taught that the truth's the best policy?

SUSPECT: Maybe I better see a lawyer. Then he can tell me what I should do.

ASSISTANT PROSECUTOR PUGLESE: You think you need an attorney to tell you whether you should tell the truth? That's a waste of money. You know it's better to level with us. We can find out. We learn things. Eventually, we'll have the truth. Why not make it easier for all of us, and tell the truth now?

SUSPECT: What's the harm if I talk to my lawyer? (*Excitedly*) I'm entitled to talk to him, ain't I? Ain't I? I got rights!

ASSISTANT PROSECUTOR PUGLESE: Sure you have. Calm down. Sure you do. But, what do you need a lawyer for now? We're just looking for the truth. If you didn't do it—tell us. If you did it—tell us. And if you didn't and you know who did—just tell us.

QUESTIONS

1. Is the use of compulsion in the police interrogation of the suspect in this case a violation of the Fifth Amendment rights, the privilege against self-incrimination?

2. Is the technique illustrated in Scene 1, the advice to plead self-defense, likely to secure a trustworthy confession?

3. Does the "friendly-unfriendly" team interrogation technique in Scene 2 threaten the validity of any subsequent confession?

4. Does the technique shown in Scene 3, in which the suspect is advised that he does not need an attorney to tell the truth (after the suspect requests an attorney), violate the Sixth Amendment's guarantee of the right to legal counsel?

SUMMARY

There are similar characteristics in the facts of the three case studies in this chapter. In the "Pot Party" case, the Fourth Amendment rights of citizens against illegal search and seizure are reviewed in opposition to the police role of arresting persons who violate laws. In the stop-and-frisk case of *Terry v. Ohio*,[9] the same citizen's rights are reviewed; but this time in opposition to the more specific police role of acting when objective reasons justify appropriate action. In the "Silent Suspect" case, the Fifth Amendment's privilege against self-incrimination is reviewed in opposition to three specific interrogation practices, and the total effect ("pressures") of this style of police questioning.

In total, the three cases reveal that judicial review has developed a body of decisional, or case, law which establishes minimal standards for police. This legal review has balanced the Fourth, Fifth, and Sixth Amendment rights of citizens against the duty of police in the investigation of crime.

While each case in this chapter focuses on specific aspects of police practice, all three cases should also be considered in light of the broader question: Should the tendency of those who execute the criminal laws of this country to obtain conviction by means of unlawful seizures and enforced confessions be sanctioned by judicial approval?[10]

[9]392 U.S. 1 (1967).
[10]Developed from the wording of the majority opinion in *Weeks v. U.S.*, 232 U.S. 383 (1914).

CHAPTER THREE

Eyewitness Identification

The common procedure of eyewitness identification presents many legal problems to police investigators. The accused is entitled to a full hearing on the identification issue at trial, and police must avoid any conduct likely to improperly influence witnesses. However, exhibiting the accused person to prosecution eyewitnesses prior to trial involves no compulsion of the accused to give testimonial evidence, in violation of the Fifth Amendment's privilege against self-incrimination. The protection of the self-incrimination privilege is applicable only to an accused's communications, whatever form they might take.[1]

There is a possibility of unfairness, seriously jeopardizing an accused's opportunity for a fair trial, in any form of out-of-court identification by eye witnesses to a crime. A conviction based on an in-court eyewitness identification at trial may be set aside on appellate review because this prior identification from photographs may be so suggestive as to prompt misidentification.[2] In-court identification by an eye witness to whom the accused was exhibited before trial in the absence of counsel is also excluded, unless it can be established that such evidence had an independent origin, or was a harmless error.[3]

The pretrial confrontation for the purpose of identification may take the form of a lineup, also known as an "identification parade" or "showup," or presentation of the suspect alone to the witness. It is obvious that risks of suggestion attend either form of confrontation, and thus

[1]*Schmerber v. California*, 384 U.S. 757 (1966).
[2]*Simmons v. U.S.*, 390 U.S. (1968), p. 384.
[3]*U.S. v. Wade*, 388 U.S. 218 (1967).

increase the dangers inherent in eyewitness identification. These confrontations probably account for many miscarriages of justice.

The first case in this chapter, Case Study No. 7, is based on the U.S. Supreme Court's decision and majority opinion in *U.S. v. Wade*.[4] This is the case in which the Court ruled that out-of-court police lineups were a "critical stage" of pretrial procedures, at which an accused was as much entitled to counsel (Sixth Amendment) as he was at the trial itself. The case study presents a brief exposition of the lineup in which Wade was identified by two eyewitnesses, not in the presence of his counsel. This lineup was the basis of Wade's petition to the U.S. Supreme Court to review his conviction. The conviction itself was based mainly on a subsequent in-court identification at the trial. As presented, this case study is not intended to explore the legal aspects of this case, but rather to present an extended reenactment of the out-of-court lineup procedures along the "story line" of the testimony of witnesses in the Wade trial. The goal of the case study is to show the potential for mistaken identification inherent in any such out-of-court confrontation between a suspect and eyewitness to a crime.

The other case in this chapter, Case Study No. 8, is concerned with a series of rapes in which eyewitness identification was mistaken, and only fortuitous circumstances prevented a miscarriage of justice.

[4]388 U.S. 218 (1967).

Billy Joe Wade

This case traces the out-of-court identification of an accused armed robber. Scene 1 presents the first identification of the accused by eyewitnesses, from photographs shown to them by investigators. Scene 2 depicts the circumstances of the out-of-court police lineup, after the accused was indicted, at which time the same eyewitnesses identified Wade in a police lineup in which Wade was a participant.

CAST OF CHARACTERS

FBI Agent   ROBERT AMOS
First Witness   VICE PRESIDENT OF BANK
Second Witness   CASHIER OF BANK
Billy Joe Wade and Other Participants in Lineup

SCENE 1: *Vice President's area in bank, adjacent to a row of teller windows. An FBI agent talks to two bank employees who have just been robbed.*

FBI AGENT: My name is Robert Amos. I'm an FBI agent. Here (*presents wallet for inspection to Bank Vice President*) are my credentials.

BANK VICE PRESIDENT: (*After looking at wallet for a moment*) Amos? I guess you are here about the robbery?

FBI AGENT: That's right. I understand you were one of the persons who got a good look at this robber while he was in the bank.

BANK VICE PRESIDENT: Yes. I'm Vice President of the bank, and I serve as operations officer. Ah! Here's our cashier now. (*Cashier enters and joins agent and Vice President*) She's the other person who was in the bank at the time. It was a real frightening experience.

CASHIER: You can say that again. He, the robber that is, had his face fixed up like war paint—like an Indian—and it gave me a scare.

FBI AGENT: (*To Cashier*) Not such a scare that you didn't look at him or would fail to recognize him again?

CASHIER: No! Certainly not! He looked scary, but after the first fright, it was just like any other nasty experience. No, I know what he looks like. I remember him. In fact, I couldn't forget him.

FBI AGENT: (*To Vice President*) I guess it was a shock to you. I hope it wasn't too much of a shock to injure your identification of this man at some future time?

BANK VICE PRESIDENT: No. I will not forget him—not for a long time. I did get a good look at him. The shock was unexpected—it was a slow day.

FBI AGENT: Now, I'd like to show you some pictures. These are what might be termed suspicious people in regard to bank robberies. We have good reasons, based on our experience in law enforcement, in selecting these photographs. The people shown in these photographs are persons who may have— let's say, may have a "potential" for robbing banks. (*Spreads out two rows of 6 or 7 photographs on the desk in front of each witness.*) I ask that you look at them carefully. Each of you have a full set of pictures. Now, without consulting with one another, select a photograph of the person you believe to be the robber, or a photo resembling such a person, or tell me that none of these photos bear any resemblance to the robber. (*Vice President and Cashier examine the "mug" shots.*) Remember, first, try to pick out the robber, then, a person like the robber, then, negative—no one looks like the robber. (*Both witnesses, in turn, review the photos and each picks one out.*) (*Agent then turns to Vice President*) Sir, have you made a decision? What do you find?

BANK VICE PRESIDENT: Yes, I have. I think I found a photo that—I think I can safely state—I found a photo I believe to be the man who robbed us, who made us put the money in the pillow case.

CASHIER: I have also. I'm sure of this man—although a lot of your photographs look a great deal alike. He's the man who shoved the dirty old pillowcase at me and said, "Put the money in the bag."

FBI AGENT: Good. That's fine. (*To Vice President*) What did you pick? (*Vice President selects a photo and hands it to agent. Agent then turns to Cashier.*) What one did you select? (*Cashier hands a photo to agent.*)

CASHIER: Is that all?

FBI AGENT: (*Looking at notebook and backs of photos, and making notes*) I think you will both be very happy to hear that each of you selected the same man. His name is Billy Joe Wade. I cannot tell you any more about him, but I would like to ask you a few more questions—

SCENE 2: *A room for witnesses to view a police lineup. Time is about six weeks later. Witnesses view lineup through a one-way screen. The witness' room is dimly lighted. The men in the lineup stand on a small stage against a ruled wall—the rulings indicate height from the floor of stage in feet and inches. There is an overhead microphone approximately in the center of the lineup stage. The FBI agent and the two witnesses from Scene 1 are present as the scene opens.*

FBI AGENT: This is nothing more than an extension of your identification of the pictures of Billy Joe Wade. He's been arrested and he'll be in this line-up. We are going to ask each of the men in the line-up to say, "Put the money in the bag," as you told us the robber said at the time of the robbery; and when all of them are through, then—not before—we will ask you each in turn to make the identification. Is that understood?

BANK VICE PRESIDENT: Don't say anything until all of them have finished speaking, is that it?

CASHIER: You don't want us to say anything until we get through this— this ceremony?

FBI AGENT: That's right. View the whole proceeding, make your decision, and let me know when I ask you. The men will each be under a number—we count from the left, the first on the left, the second, etc. Let's (*loudly*) get on with it. (*The lineup room lights go on. Five people can be seen on the lineup stage. All of them have tape strips on their faces running horizontally, from ear to nose and mouth.*)

BANK VICE PRESIDENT: Okay.

CASHIER: I'm ready.

FBI AGENT: (*Into small hand microphone*) First man, let's hear it. You have had your instructions. Say "Put the money in the bag."

FIRST MAN IN LINEUP: (*Reluctantly*) Put the money in the bag.

SECOND MAN IN LINEUP: (*Rapidly*) Put the money in the bag.

FBI AGENT: Wait— Hold it up. Talk when I tell you to— Please.

SECOND MAN IN LINEUP: Okay, put the money in the bag.

THIRD MAN IN LINEUP: (*Slowly*) Put the money in the bag.

FOURTH MAN IN LINEUP: Put the cash in the bag. I mean, put the money in the bag.

FIFTH MAN IN LINEUP: (*Very low*) Put the money in it.

FBI AGENT: Come on. (*very loudly*) Put the money in the bag.

FIFTH MAN IN LINEUP: (*Very loudly*) Put the money in the bag.

FBI AGENT: (*Turns to witnesses and holds hand over microphone*) All right, you have seen them all, now what do you say?

BANK VICE PRESIDENT: Number three, no doubt about it. No doubt—None—

CASHIER: Number three, also. I can never forget—

FBI AGENT: Thank you, thank you. All right (*into microphone*), hold number three. We won't need the others.

QUESTIONS

1.   Will the results of this out-of-court identification settle the fate of the man identified, and reduce the trial itself to a mere formality?

2.   Is there a cumulative suggestibility factor in this identification procedure which threatens the integrity of any subsequent in-court identification?

3.   Are the accused's Sixth Amendment rights (right to confront witnesses and assistance of counsel) violated by this prior identification through photographs and appearance in a lineup without aid of a lawyer?

Three Rapes

This series of rapes happened in quick succession, in a city of over 200,000, and in a residential area centered on the campus of a state college with a student body of 10,000 and a faculty of 700 instructors. The case study follows the chronological progress of these three crimes; the first arrest and hearing; and the second arrest and subsequent action by the prosecutor.

CRIME 1

The first crime occurred at 12:30 P.M., March 12. The victim was a twenty-seven-year-old business-woman living with her sister in an upper apartment in a two-story apartment house in a middle-income neighborhood. The victim said that the perpetrator, to gain entry, posed as a college student conducting a field survey. She described him as a white male, in his early twenties, 6'1" in height, 185 pounds, medium build, brown hair (cut medium length), brown eyes, fair complexion, and dressed in a jacket and pants. Color of pants could not be recalled by the victim, but she believed that the jacket was tan or brown. No vehicle was noted by the victim; no weapon was observed.

The victim arrived at her apartment at about 12:10 P.M., for lunch. At approximately 12:50 P.M. she heard her doorbell ring. She opened her door, and a young man in his early twenties was standing just outside the door. He told the victim that he was doing a survey for a course that he was taking in college. He asked the victim several questions. Two of the questions were: "Is the Johnson poverty program practical?" and "Should we pull out of Vietnam?" After several more questions, he said "Thank you very much for your help." He asked the victim her name, religion, and the state in which she was born. He then asked for a glass of water. The victim replied that she would get him the water, and as she started toward the kitchen, he followed her. Just after she entered the kitchen, he grabbed her around the neck with his arm and pressed something sharp to her throat. He then said, "All I want is money. I need money, and I won't hurt you."

The victim states that at this point, her attacker pushed a cloth gag in her mouth and asked, "Where is your money?" She pointed toward the hallway. The attacker dragged the victim into the hallway, and while she opened a drawer in a chest, he took a belt from a closet, and strapped her hands together behind her back. He then dragged her to the bedroom and placed her on the bed. He put a blindfold over her eyes, using a scarf that he had taken from a dresser in the bedroom for the blindfold.

The attacker then raised the victim's sweater, broke the strap on her brassiere and the straps on her slip, and lowered them, exposing her breasts. Then he raised the victim's skirt, removed her panties and had sexual intercourse with her. After the act was completed, the attacker dragged the still blindfolded victim to her bathroom and washed himself. Then he forced the victim to lie on the floor of the bathroom, tied her legs together, and left the apartment.

During this period, the attacker made several threats, stating that if the victim called the police, he would return and kill her. After a few minutes, the victim was able to free herself, and she called her family physician. She told him what had happened, and made an appointment for an examination at 3 P.M. She stated that the reason she did not call the police first was that she was afraid to because of her attacker's threats.

CRIME 2

The second crime occurred about two weeks later, on April 5, shortly after 2:00 P.M. The victim was a thirty-two-year-old housewife living in a lower apartment of a two-story building in an upper-middle-income neighborhood. The victim described the perpetrator as a white male, twenty-five years old, about 5'10" or 5'11", about 165 pounds, of slight build, and good-looking. The attacker posed as a college student conducting a field survey for a political science class. The object of the crime was sexual, although robbery may have been the original objective. No motor vehicle was observed. The weapon, a knife, was displayed to the victim.

The victim responded to the ringing of the doorbell and found a young white male who said he was a college student—a political science major doing a survey as part of his class work. He asked questions about

Vietnam, and after finishing the interview, which the victim said took about three to five minutes, he asked for a glass of water. The victim did not ask him in, but said she would get it for him. While at the kitchen sink, getting the water, the victim felt something (a handkerchief) being pushed into her mouth, and a knife was displayed to her by the young man. She was told not to scream, and that she wouldn't be hurt—it was money he was after. The victim does not recall his exact words.

The victim was then taken into her bedroom, thirty feet from the kitchen, where the attacker took some stockings from a dresser, made her lie face down on the bed, and tied her hands behind her back with the stockings. He then got her up on her feet, led her around the bed to the windows and pulled the shades down. He pushed her back on the bed, and said, "No money, might as well have some fun." The victim was dressed in skirt, sweater, slip, panties and brassiere. The perpetrator pulled her skirt up and her pants down. The victim held her knees together, but the attacker pushed between them, shoving her pants further down, and off, with the toe of his right shoe. The victim said that she got her hands free and struggled to one side; but her attacker put his knife under her breast and threatened her, saying, "I'll cut your tit off." He reached down, recovered the victim's panties and put them over her head as a blindfold, and had intercourse with her. After finishing, the attacker pushed the pants into her mouth as a gag. The victim thinks she was screaming, and he just pushed them in from where they were over her face. Then, the attacker took the victim into the bathroom, where he washed, and told victim not to "tell," saying that he wouldn't spend much time in jail, and that he would dynamite her house when he got out, or "get" her children or husband if she "told." He left her, saying he was going to look for money through the house, and told her not to move. She doesn't know how long she stayed there, or when the attacker did leave the house. The victim called her husband at work. The husband rushed home and called the police.

Police Investigation: Crimes 1 and 2

The victims of both crimes were shown hundreds of photographs of known local criminals. The first victim was uncooperative. However, a few days after the second crime, the victim of this second attack picked out a photograph of a young man, twenty-three years old, who had been previously convicted of the robbery of a local store and was presently on parole. His name was John Stein, and he was 6′, 170 pounds, with brown eyes and brown hair. At the time of the identification, the victim said she was "bothered" by the fact that the photograph showed a person with "pock marks" on his face, and her attacker did not have them. After Stein's arrest, on April 13, the arresting officer asked the jailer to select men of the same general physical description as given by the victim at the time of the crime, and the victim-witness of crime number 2 viewed this lineup. She picked Stein out of this group, saying that he "could be" the man, but that she was not entirely certain. The case was prepared for trial and presented to the prosecutor.

Action by Prosecutor

An assistant prosecutor was assigned, and the case was moved to a preliminary hearing in lieu of an indictment. At this hearing, the victim of the second crime was asked to step down from the witness stand and identify the man who attacked her. She confronted the defendant, Stein, who was seated at a table with his legal counsel. She studied him, and said she couldn't be sure. The prosecution placed the arresting officer on the stand. He detailed the circumstances of the lineup at which the victim-witness, who had just testified, had picked the defendant out of a group of six prisoners of similar size and appearance. The magistrate held the defendant to answer for trial.

CRIME 3

The third crime occurred on April 20, while Stein was in jail. The victim was a twenty-year-old housewife living in a middle-income neighborhood. She described the perpetrator as a white male about twenty-four years of age, about 5' 10" to 6', 170 to 180 pounds, with tan slacks and a short-sleeved, red-checked shirt. Again, the attacker claimed to be a college student conducting a political science survey. The object of attack: rape. The weapon: a pocket knife displayed to the victim and pressed to her face. No vehicle was observed.

The victim said she had returned to her apartment from shopping at 2:20 P.M., and a few minutes later, someone knocked on the door. She opened it, and a young man carrying a student-style looseleaf notebook said he would like to ask her six questions. She agreed, and he asked her questions concerning national politics, and concluded by asking her age, religion, and occupation. Then, according to the victim, he asked for a drink of water. She said she walked to the kitchen, unaware she was being followed, until suddenly, as she stood at the kitchen sink, she felt an arm thrown around her neck and saw and felt a small pocketknife pressed against her face.

The victim said she was forced by this man into her bedroom, where he shoved a handkerchief into her mouth, and tied her hands behind her back with stockings from the top of her dresser. The attacker pushed her down on the bed and placed a stocking and a hair-dryer bag—also secured from the top of the dresser—over her head and eyes, pulled her dress and underwear from her and raped her.

Afterward, the attacker took the victim into the dining room, where he tied her feet with one of her husband's ties as she lay on the floor. He placed a paring knife that he secured from the kitchen, alongside her, and said that she could use it to free herself after he left. He then warned her that he would return and kill her if she notified her husband or the police.

The victim managed to cut herself loose, went to her husband at his nearby place of business, and the two of them went to the sheriff's office to report the attack.

FIGURE 5 Identification photos of suspects 1 and 2. Suspect 1 was arrested after the first two crimes; suspect 2 was apprehended after the third crime which was committed while suspect 1 was in jail.

Police Investigation and Reinvestigation

Five days after the third crime, a U.S. Air Force enlisted man was arrested. The suspect, August Flack, had no prior arrests, was twenty-three years old, 5′ 11″, with brown eyes and hair. He confessed to be the attacker in all three crimes and was positively identified by the victim of crime number 2, who had previously identified the first arrestee (Stein). The victims of crimes 1 and 3 were uncooperative and refused to view Flack to corroborate his confession.

Action by Prosecutor

Reexamination of the case against defendant Stein resulted in a motion by the prosecutor to dismiss the case against him in the interests of justice. The examining magistrate approved the application, and the charges against Stein were dismissed. A case was then prepared to prosecute defendant Flack for the three rapes.

QUESTIONS

1. Was the first arrest in this series of crimes, the arrest of John Stein, justified?
2. What was the compelling evidence in this series of crimes that indicated the innocence of defendant Stein?
3. Was the identification process in this case (photos, lineup) an important factor in the case against Stein?

SUMMARY

The case of Billy Joe Wade illustrates the prevailing police practices in the identification of suspects by eyewitnesses to a crime. That entire procedure, which was based on the facts and testimony at Wade's trial for bank robbery, was later judged by the U.S. Supreme Court to be inherently suggestive.[5] In the Three Rapes case study, the facts of a real-life case of mistaken identification are detailed. The prompt arrest of the real offender, after the third rape, alerted police to the fact they had arrested the wrong man for the first two crimes.

Both of these cases share the theme of mistaken identification. In Wade, there is the possibility of mistaken identification, and the threat this poses to a fair trial. In the Three Rapes case, it is a mistaken identification which led police to an erroneous conclusion that the first suspect was guilty. Both cases raise the issue of the validity and reliability of eyewitness identification of suspects in criminal cases.

[5]*U.S. v. Wade*, 388 U.S. 218 (1967).

CHAPTER FOUR

Informants and Undercover Agents

When an eyewitness is not available to assist in the identification of the perpetrator of a crime, or when criminal operations are hidden and secret (as in the selling of narcotics, prostitution, arson, theft, conspiracy to commit crime, etc.), police have traditionally employed informants and undercover agents for the purpose of securing information about persons involved in crime. The information collected by police from these secret sources may prompt an investigation, expose a crime, provide sufficient information to warrant an arrest or search, and even provide sufficient data to arrest and prosecute a person or group of persons.[1]

Courts recognize the need for police to utilize informants and to keep the identity of these individuals secret. It is considered to be in the public interest to protect this flow of data about crime and criminals. However, a person accused of crime is entitled to a full and fair opportunity to defend himself. Therefore, while the identity of secret sources of information is generally protected, the scope of the privilege not to disclose an informant's identity depends on the particular circumstances of each case: the crime charged, the possible defenses, the significance of the informant's testimony, and other relevant factors. Once disclosure is required by the court, the prosecution must comply with the court's order, or the criminal action will be dismissed.

Undercover agents are usually law enforcement personnel who are not known to the local underworld. Unlike informants, whose credibility is often suspect because of their criminal histories or association with criminals, the undercover police agent is a person of good reputation and char-

---

[1]Wayne R. LaFave, *Arrest: The Decision to Take a Suspect into Custody* (Boston: Little Brown, 1965), pp. 265–74.

acter, a "sworn" agent of law enforcement assigned to this type of work. The methodology of police use of undercover agents is to protect the agent's identity while he is collecting "intelligence"—data transmitted for interpretation and dissemination by others—or developing a case for prosecution. Then, police usually disclose the agent's identity when an arrest is made.[2] This is generally termed "burning up" an undercover agent. He can no longer perform this type of work once his identity has been disclosed. Police expect to make such a disclosure, as they are well aware that the agent's testimony is usually vital to a successful prosecution, and the agent must reveal himself in order to testify.

The first two cases in this chapter, Case Studies 9 and 10, are concerned with police use of informants. In Case Study 9, the facts of *McCray v. Illinois*[3] have been adapted to develop the issue of whether the informant's identity is necessary for an adequate defense. *McCray* is a landmark case in the area of the "informant privilege." However, this case study is not planned to detail the many intricacies of case law in this area. Its goal is to reveal the balance that must be sought between the public interest in protecting the identity of informants and the defendant's right to ask for the disclosure of an informant's identity, when it is necessary for a fair determination of his guilt or innocence. This is usually the issue in these cases. Case Study 10 discloses the facts of an arrest in which the accused claimed that his role as a police informant warranted his possession of forty-seven "lids" of marijuana.

The final case in this chapter, Case Study 11, details the role of an undercover agent in an extensive investigation of arson and murder. This is the story of the "Molly Maguires" of the Pennsylvania coal fields. The time is the last half of the nineteenth century. The issue in this case is not the identity of the undercover private police agent; but it is the fundamental fairness and merit of this methodology of collecting evidence.[4]

[2]Paul B. Weston and Kenneth M. Wells, *Criminal Investigation: Basic Perspectives* (Englewood Cliffs, N.J.: Prentice-Hall, 1970), pp. 172–74.

[3]386 U.S. 300 (1967).

[4]Francis P. Dewees, *The Molly Maguires* (New York: Burt Franklin, 1966), pp. 45–79.

McCray and the Reliable Informant

The *McCray* case was one of a long line of cases which had been the subject of courtroom debate as to whether or not the identity of a police informant should be disclosed to guarantee a defendant his right to a fair trial. However, at the time of McCray's petition to the U.S. Supreme Court for review, the Court believed it was an appropriate case and an appropriate time to review this issue. The case is presented in a conversational style, with the action taking place in the judicial chambers of an appellate court judge. The scene and its dialogue is quite unusual, but it does simplify the *McCray* story, and the Court's decision and majority opinion in this case.

CAST OF CHARACTERS

Narrator ANONYMOUS OBSERVER
Judge A JUSTICE OF AN APPELLATE COURT
Prosecutor ANONYMOUS
Defense Attorney ANONYMOUS
Defendant GEORGE MCCRAY

SCENE 1: *Judicial chambers, the judge is still in his robe, but is relaxed in a swivel chair behind a massive desk. Two persons, the prosecutor and the defense attorney, are seated in front of the desk. The narrator is unseen.*

NARRATOR: George McCray, the defendant in this case, was identified to the arresting officers, by an informant, as a person who sold drugs. On the day of the arrest, the informant told the arresting officers that McCray was now "holding"—had drugs—and could be found nearby (at 47th Street and Calumet Avenue) at that time. The officers went to this location, and observed McCray talking with several persons. The individuals would approach McCray, talk a short time, and then walk away. The officers tried to get closer, to observe if anything was being passed to these people during these conversations. McCray was alert. He noticed them, and started to walk hurriedly away. When they saw they had been discovered, the officers moved, seized McCray, placed him under arrest, and searched him. The major evidence at McCray's subsequent trial was the narcotics found on his person during this arrest-based search. McCray was convicted, sentenced, and is now appealing his conviction.

JUDGE: Gentlemen, I'm certain you know that in our review, as an appellate tribunal, we must be mindful of the Fourth Amendment's command that a judicial mind must be interposed between the police and the citizen in determining the validity of a proposed arrest; and we must —as a court of review—be equally attentive to the need for disclosing an informant's identity, when the informant is an active participant in the crime, and when his testimony is material to the issue of the guilt or innocence of the defendant.

PROSECUTOR: Let us remember that one of the arresting officers testified at McCray's trial that he had known the informant for close to a year, that during this period the informant had given him information about 15 times—all relating to drug-selling—and that all of this information was found to be accurate and resulted in arrests and convictions. This officer gave the court names and dates of arrests and convictions that were based on the informant's information. This should be significant, and it is all in the record.

JUDGE: I'm sure there was other validation of this informant as a reliable one. The reliability of an informant must be shown by affirmative evidence—

PROSECUTOR (*Interrupting*): Yes, your Honor. Another officer testified that he had known this informant for about two years, and that he had received information from him twenty or thirty times, and that this information had resulted in convictions.

JUDGE: Convictions? How many convictions? Are we safe in assuming that you mean twenty or thirty convictions?

DEFENSE ATTORNEY: That is a very unsafe assumption. The record shows that when this officer was queried on cross-examination he had a memory lapse as to the exact number of convictions. He just summed up that he had found him to be an informant from whom he got results, and this he said meant convictions.

PROSECUTOR: I don't know, your Honor. I'll disagree until I check the court transcript. What defense counsel states may be true. My recall is that the officer testified to the use of this informant, and then I believe his words were: "This information resulted in convictions."

JUDGE: Thank you, gentlemen. It's not any clearer, but I think the record will reveal this important point when we review the trial court transcript.

DEFENSE ATTORNEY: Your Honor, the due process clause of the Fourteenth Amendment guarantees that rights that constitute "due process" will be given to defendants in state courts; yet my client's right under the Sixth Amendment—to be confronted by sworn witnesses available for cross examination—has been nullified in this case.

JUDGE: As I understand it, your claim is that an informant's identity needs to be disclosed to determine whether the arresting officers had sufficient probable cause for an arrest.

DEFENSE ATTORNEY: Yes, your Honor. Since the major item of evidence was narcotics seized during an arrest-based search, it is important to my client's defense that we establish that the officer did *not* have sufficient probable cause to justify an arrest, and thus make the resultant search an illegal one, which would justify suppressing the evidence against my client. To do so we should have had disclosure of the informant's identity, and an opportunity to cross-examine him as to what he did tell the arresting officers, and the truthfulness of his and their statements.

JUDGE: Appellate courts have consistently declined to hold that an informant's identity need always be disclosed. This might shut off the flow of information to police which is vital to their work, and thus destroy much of their effectiveness in criminal investigation. I know you are both aware of this, and also that when the individual circumstances warrant disclosure, any court of review will be forthright in so ordering it.

PROSECUTOR: The arresting officers in this case testified, in open court, fully and in precise detail, as to what the informant had told them, and why they had reason to believe that this information was trustworthy. Each of the two arresting officers was under oath when he so testified, and each was available for, and subjected to, a searching cross-examination!

JUDGE: True—and we've had a nice talk—but (*rising to indicate dismissal*) does the trial court transcript indicate that the trial judge was apparently satisfied that these officers were telling the truth?

DEFENSE ATTORNEY: That— Yes— That is the reason that he exercised his discretion to overrule my objections at the trial, and that he didn't respond to my demands—motions, that is—that the state be forced to produce the informer to testify, and to be available for cross-examination. You realize, (*rises*) your Honor, if I may, that our cross-examination of the arresting officers was restricted by this refusal to identify the informant?

PROSECUTOR: (*Rises and moves away from the desk*) A fine judge, one of the best—

JUDGE: Rest assured, gentlemen, that the court, all of us, will examine this claim.

NARRATOR: The court's decision in *McCray v. Illinois* upheld the police and prosecutor's reluctance to disclose the identity of the informant in this case, and the trial judge's refusal to force disclosure. The court's opinion stated that information from a reliable informant supplied sufficient probable cause for making an arrest; and that there was no need to disclose the identity of the informant on this issue of probable cause. Therefore, the arrest was legal. Thus, the search was a legal and reasonable search, and the fruits of that search were properly admitted into evidence against McCray at his trial for possession of narcotics in violation of the law.

QUESTIONS

1. Was the court's decision to protect the identity of the informant in this case justified?

2. Was the fact that the informant's testimony was not material to the issue of the guilt or innocence of the defendant a major factor in the court's decision?

3. On the issue of whether the use of an informant in this case was a "shabby thing"[5] (an undesirable police technique), do the facts given indicate that the arresting officer could have made this arrest without the use of an informant?

[5]*Hoffa v. U.S.*, 385 U.S. 293 (1966), at p. 311.

Forty-Seven "Lids" of Marijuana

The single scene in this case study is a courtroom. The participants are the classic trio usually present at the original arraignment of a defendant, his first court appearance after an arrest: a judge, an arresting officer, and the defendant. The defendant has attempted to excuse his illegal possession of marijuana by claiming to be a police informant. The case study omits most of the routine of these hearings: the judicial advice to the defendant about his constitutional rights and court procedure, the reading of the "complaint" listing the crime charged, and the testimony of the arresting officer in support of his summary arrest of the defendant. It begins almost at the close of the hearing. In this fashion the full impact of the judicial reasoning on the merits of the case is emphasized.

CAST OF CHARACTERS

Judge ANONYMOUS
Police Officer ROBERT HOLBROOK
Defendant ANTHONY LEDENT

SCENE 1: *Courtroom—a prisoner is being arraigned. He stands beside a police officer in plainclothes. Both men are facing the judge's bench. The time is a day after the prisoner was arrested. There has been previous testimony in the case, and the presiding judge is reviewing the facts and testimony just presented in court.*

JUDGE: This forty-seven "lids" of marijuana— That is quite a substantial, what is it, "stash"? (*Defendant and officer nod in agreement.*)

OFFICER: It is a wholesale quantity, no doubt.

DEFENDANT: They told me to keep selling. I had to have supplies.

JUDGE: Let me sum up, for my own understanding, what we have heard so far: (*To defendant*) Your defense is that you possessed this quantity of drugs illegally, under the exception to the Penal Code allowing temporary incidental possession by persons whose possession is for the purpose of aiding public officers—police and narcotic agents—in performing their official duties, and that Lieutenant Friend, in charge of the vice detail for the city police, asked you to inform on the drug scene —to give him information. Is that true?

DEFENDANT: Well, I went to the lieutenant. I had been arrested for possession. They had me dead to rights. Some one of my customers blew the whistle on me. I sent out word from the jail that I wanted to see him—Lieutenant Friend—and that I could help him get better arrests than—

JUDGE: (*Interrupting*) You and Lieutenant Friend, in his official capacity did talk; and you and he agreed that you would function as an informant of some kind. Is that true?

DEFENDANT: Yes, but he don't give me any money. He don't say, "Here's a C note, go out and make a buy." What we understood, him and I, was that I was to buy and sell, and carry on like I had done before—

OFFICER: (*Interrupting*) I'm a deputy sheriff, your Honor, but I don't think any police lieutenant in the city would allow that—

DEFENDANT: (*Interrupting*) Judge, my lawyer on the first rap, he got it ironed out. I was discharged on it for lack of evidence, is what it said— but really it was because I agreed to cooperate—

JUDGE: I have here a court disposition (*reading*) that states your case was disposed of by an examining magistrate, and that you were not held to answer. There was a lack of evidence, apparently; but if you tell me now that there was collusion here to compromise this crime and to conceal evidence in order to threaten you, or to bargain with you—

DEFENDANT: Judge—we all sit down: my lawyer, the lieutenant, and the Assistant DA that has my case. They promised to drop the charges in exchange for information.

JUDGE: I shall look into that—Now, let's get on here. There has been testimony here today that this evidence was seized pursuant to a search warrant, and the officer has made a return to the court on the warrant in which he states that forty-seven "lids" of marijuana were found in the possession of the defendant. The defendant is held to answer as charged. I cannot reasonably find from the evidence, that the possession of forty-seven "lids" of marijuana, a wholesale quantity of this drug, was for the purpose of aiding public officers in performing their official duties. The defendant is held for appearance and trial in Superior Court. You have an attorney, I believe you said, that is coming into this case?

DEFENDANT: Yes, I have. He could of been here today, but—

JUDGE: It wasn't necessary. His turn will come later—to prove this story of yours (*rising and picking up papers*); and I am going to look into it. I cannot bring myself to believe that any law enforcement officer would encourage anyone to possess forty-seven "lids" of an illegal drug such as marijuana, for the purpose of serving as an informant.

QUESTIONS

1.   On the facts of this case, was the decision of the judge justified?
2.   Was the quantity of marijuana found in the possession of defendant the major contributing factor in the court's decision?
3.   On the issue of whether the use of informants is a desirable police technique, do the facts of this case indicate that the recruitment and use of informants such as Ledent, the defendant in this case, threaten the integrity of this process of using underworld informants?

The Molly Maguires and the Pinkertons

During the period from 1840 to 1880 numerous social and economic problems resulted from the operation of coal mines in eastern Pennsylvania. While the elements of strife included Democrat against Republican, immigrant against native American, and Protestant against Catholic, the major quarrel developed between labor and management; miners and the owners of coal mines.

Rudimentary labor "locals" sought to protect the miners from low wages and unsafe working conditions, but they were strongly opposed by the employers. Secret groups, organized to conceal affiliation with any labor organization, were organized to protect the rights of the miners. These groups were crude and rough, and sometimes lawless, but their general objectives were related to resolving legitimate labor problems. Wages paid to miners fluctuated from year to year, but they were determined by the minimum price at which labor could be hired. From 1840 to 1860, a wage of $1.05 a day was average in the Pennsylvania coal fields, but there was no guarantee of a living wage over a long period of time. A surplus of labor and the absence of an effective labor organization made possible the dictation of wages by employers. The employers also rented housing to the miners and operated a "company store." Men were known to work in the mines and receive no more than a "bobtail check": a statement indicating the miner had no wages due at the end of the month; rent and groceries purchased at the company store had exceeded earnings.[6]

[6]J. Walter Coleman, *The Molly Maguire Riots—Industrial Conflict in the Pennsylvania Coal Region* (New York: Arno and the New York Times, 1969), pp. 1–18.

Among the exploited miners were a good percentage of Irish immigrants. Famine-ridden Ireland contributed to the labor surplus in the Pennsylvania coal fields. By the middle of the eighteenth century the Irish comprised the majority of residents in many areas of the anthracite region. In this region the Democratic Party now relied on the Irish miners for support. The Molly Maguires[6a] first surfaced as a secret society identified with the Irish, the Democratic Party, and resistance to the 1862 draft. Voluntary enlistments had failed to recruit an army sufficient to continue the year-old Civil War. Andrew Curtain, Pennsylvania's governor, was a Republican and a strong pro-Unionist, but he recognized the disenchantment of the miners with the war and pleaded with federal officials to avoid any conflict with the miners in enforcing the draft quotas, saying that the draft could not be executed in the anthracite region without a bloody conflict with the Molly Maguires. Draft disturbances in 1862 and 1863 produced violence in the coal fields, but major confrontations between troops and resisters were avoided by trick bookkeeping which gave the appearance of enforcing the draft.[7]

At the end of the Civil War, the market for coal fell, miners' wages were reduced, and unemployment increased in the coal regions. Except for weak locals of employees, the miners had no union to represent their interests. The Molly Maguires became a political group because hundreds of men living in the towns and villages in the coal fields belonged to this secret society; they became a strong labor group because most of these members were miners or merchants friendly to the working class. As a group, they used force and violence, but often in response to violence on the part of the operators of the coal mines and the men hired to protect mines and railroads. In 1865, the Pennsylvania legislature enacted legislation permitting the formation of a private police force: the "Coal and Iron Police." In theory, the organization's powers were limited to property protection. In practice, there was no limit to the powers usurped by the Coal and Iron Police. New recruits were told their first duty was to their employers, the railroad and mining corporations that did the hiring.[8]

The controversy between the owners of the coal mines and the railroads and the coal miners led to an increasing amount of violence. Authorities at local and state levels termed the acts part of a criminal conspiracy. The victims in each case were identified with the management of the coal mines; the suspects were described as members of an Irish group

[6a]Named after a nebulous figure in Irish folklore known for her leadership of an underground group in Ireland who followed the precepts of Robin Hood: take from the rich and give to the poor.

[7]Wayne G. Broehl, Jr., *The Molly Maguires* (Cambridge: Harvard University Press, 1964), pp. 85–93.

[8]Arthur H. Lewis, *Lament for the Molly Maguires* (New York: Harcourt Brace Jovanovich, 1964), pp. 33–37.

of miners particularly dissatisfied with the low wages and working conditions in the coal fields of this region.

In the tradition of American policing at that time, large rewards were offered for the arrest and conviction of the persons who were assaulting and killing management personnel of the mines. Private detectives in the employ of coal companies were deputized as members of the "Coal and Iron Police" to assist local police officers. However, no effective police measure was found. The crimes went on. They were not only unchecked—they continued to increase steadily.[9]

There was no evidence that this rash of crimes in the Pennsylvania coal mine country were committed because of the usual motivation of professional or accidental criminals. On the other hand, there was evidence that the crimes were designed to harrass the owners and operators of the coal mines into sharing a greater amount of the profits of coal mining with the workers in the mines.

Police in the area believed the crimes to be part of a criminal conspiracy sponsored by the Molly Maguires, and that the Mollies were a select group within the framework of the Irish benevolent association, The Ancient Order of Hibernians.

The Molly Maguires surfaced by name in a labor dispute in 1862. About two hundred men, armed with guns and other weapons, attacked a colliery in Cass Township. They wrecked machinery, beat workers and closed up the colliery store. They closed down operations, remained at the scene for about two hours, identified themselves as "the Molly Maguires," and warned that a reopening of the colliery would lead to another attack.

The Molly Maguires were a formal and organized organization in that there was a division of labor, individual activities were coordinated through planning and executive direction, and all operations were designed to achieve the organization's specific objectives. Therefore, the Molly Maguires had goals, procedures, and a structure not common to burglars, thieves, and other professional criminals.

Many of the homicides were preceded by so-called "coffin notices" which were threats by the Molly Maguires that called for either a cease-and-desist action in regard to some management practice, or contained an order to leave the vicinity by a certain time and date. Later, it was discovered that these notices were not issued at the whim of anyone in the Molly Maguire hierarchy, but were the product of some rudimentary hearing, at which the action was discussed by a group of members and decided upon only if a majority vote to take the suggested action was secured.

The murder of a "boss" at the colliery at Raven's Run is illustrative of the operations of a Molly Maguire execution committee. Thomas Sanger had been marked for death—a coffin notice tacked on his door. The killer

[9]Coleman, *The Molly Maguire Riots,* pp. 70–74, 168–75.

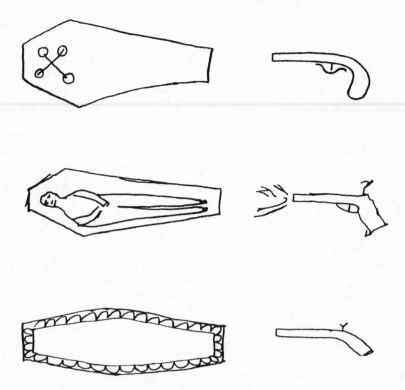

FIGURE 6   The "coffin notice" of the Molly Maguires were threatening notes to coal mine management personnel. They contained crude drawings of coffins and guns to emphasize the threat of death.

team arrived in Raven's Run about 6 A.M., and concealed themselves in a crowd of over a hundred miners who were waiting to go to work. At about 6:30 A.M., Sanger appeared from the colliery office to assign work to the men on the day shift. An assistant, William Uren, walked at his side and they began to assign the workers. Then Sanger and Uren were shot by one of a five-man team. The four other "Mollies" fired into the crowd of workmen, stampeding them from the area. Sanger, who had fallen, ran toward a nearby residence. He was chased by several of the Mollies and shot again. The attackers then fled into the nearby woods. Sanger and Uren died within hours—neither could identify any attacker.

Franklin B. Gowen was one of the mine-owners of that period. He was president of the Philadelphia and Reading Railroad Company, and owner-operator of the Philadelphia Coal and Iron Company. He was born in Philadelphia in 1836. His father had been born in Ireland, but immigrated to the United States as a young man, settling in Philadelphia where he prospered as a merchant. Franklin was educated at a private academy in Philadelphia. Later, his education and family background allowed him to enter the coal business at the age of twenty-one, in 1858, as a full partner in a successful business firm.

In 1860, Gowen gave up business to study law, and he soon established a practice serving large landowners—including the wealthy Girard family of Philadelphia. In 1862, he was elected District Attorney of Schuylkill County in the center of the coal-mining area. During his incumbency in this office of criminal justice, Gowen was appointed counsel for the Philadelphia and Reading Railroad Company. His financial holdings in the coal fields were pyramided around this time, when Gowen organized the Philadelphia Coal and Iron Company to acquire coal-mine properties. In 1869, he accepted the presidency of the Philadelphia and Reading Railroad Company.

As a coal-mine operator, and as legal counsel for other owner-operators, Franklin B. Gowen viewed the activities of the Molly Maguires as a threat and encroachment upon property rights. As a prosecutor and a citizen of the area, he knew of the reign of terror of the Mollies, and he knew that the ordinary machinery of law enforcement and criminal justice was helpless in the face of their organized criminal operations. As a concerned member of the community, Gowen sought counsel and advice from others in the community who had similar interests in the control of crime. As a business man, he no doubt consulted with associates, and possibly with competitors, since the activities of the Molly Maguires threatened the entire structure of management in this business of mining, transportation, and selling coal.

There has been controversy over the years about Franklin B. Gowen's motivation for bringing in privately-employed police, and the new police techniques that were used to combat the Molly Maguires. On the one hand, there is the claim that Gowen was a union-buster, and to maintain his way of life, and the value of his investments, he fought against the Molly Maguires as part of a larger war against the unionization of workingmen which he believed was threatening his profits. On the other hand, it is alleged that Gowen was just fed up, as a citizen and a member of the community, with the brutal outrages committed upon casually selected victims, and with the police behavior which lacked the inventiveness and innovation necessary to secure results.

In any event, Franklin B. Gowen sought help. He solicited the special interest of Alan Pinkerton, the founder of the Pinkerton Detective Agency. The Pinkertons, or the "Pinks" as they were also known, had recently begun to operate nationally, with an effectiveness never developed by local police groups. They were under contract, at the time, to Gowen's P & R Railroad—to detect pilferage among the train conductors, and they were under contract to Gowen's coal company for the physical security of the collieries.

Allan Pinkerton was of Scottish birth. He received training as a cooper, emigrated to the United States in 1843, secured employment in his trade in Illinois, but left it to join the Chicago Police Department. In his early police service, Pinkerton distinguished himself in criminal investigation. He was one of the first detectives assigned full-time to this work in Chicago. Friendships that he developed in his work led him to leave police service and open his private detection service in 1850. The success of the Pinkertons has been described as based on giving service to their clients. Summed up, this means getting results.

Pinkerton developed an innovative idea in criminal investigation into a going business. This was to reject the existing informant system used by the police, and in its place substitute a system of gaining data based on trustworthy undercover agents. The "Pinks" became an agency organized to do intelligence work, and to report to their clients the intelligence collected. When a case was developed to a point where there was a potential for arrest, Allan Pinkerton favored the interdiction of the criminal in the act of a crime. This was possible when the collected intelligence indicated when and where the next crime was likely to be committed. He also favored a tireless and relentless pursuit when a criminal was identified as a major suspect in a crime in which his agents had collected legally significant evidence.

Up until the time of the Molly Maguire case, Pinkerton had never been known to expose the operations of an undercover agent by allowing such an employee to testify to his collected intelligence at the trial of an offender. It is more than likely that the businessman in Allan Pinkerton just did not relish the idea of destroying the usefulness of a trained and ex-experienced agent by public exposure of his identity. This would be necessary if such agent had to serve as a witness in a criminal proceeding. It may be that Mr. Pinkerton, as an old police detective, believed that the intelligence that he offered police and prosecutors furnished the necessary promising leads to develop their own cases without any great difficulty.

Pinkerton found nothing morally wrong in using deceit to detect criminals and criminal operations. He did not subscribe to the belief that entire honesty of word and deed is essential to morality. In fact, he strongly believed that no one can complain of being wronged if he is detected in the commission of a crime, or if he is revealed as a person who has committed a past crime—no matter what methods of detection were used.

Pinkerton's undercover agent in the Molly Maguire case was a young Irishman named James McParlan. McParlan developed a cover story in line with his ethnic background and previous work experience. The story was that McParlan was a fugitive from justice. He successfully infiltrated the Molly Maguire organization, gained the confidence of the ringleaders, and filed almost daily reports direct to the Pinkerton Agency in Philadelphia. He skirted actually becoming involved as a principal, or an accessory, in any of the crimes of the Molly Maguires, and when Allan Pinkerton made the decision to turn over the collected intelligence to agents of law enforcement, McParlan was recalled and assigned to other duties by Pinkerton.

Despite definitive data on the specifics of each crime and the names and roles of each participant, which were supplied by McParlan's reports, local prosecutors and their police investigators could not overcome the reluctance of witnesses to talk. They failed to develop a state's witness from among the co-conspirators, and they reported that the prosecution of any individual case was threatened by the classic alibi defense of the Molly Maguire organization.

Gowen and Pinkerton met in executive session. The decision was to "burn up" McParlan—to sacrifice him as a useful undercover agent by disclosing his identity and operations. The strength of the Pinkertons under the leadership of Alan Pinkerton may be indicated by the fact that McParlan was a willing witness despite the fact that he might be "signing his own death warrant," and despite his expressed disinclination to accept the public role of informer.

McParlan's testimony at various trials for murder led to the conviction of the leader of the Molly Maguires, several lieutenants, and all of the members of the organization's execution squads. The secret organization, and its code of silence, had been broken by an undercover agent. When McParlan spoke out in open court, and weathered day after day of scathing cross-examination on the witness stand, the alibi defense of the conspirators was smashed because the juries believed the man from the Pinkerton Agency.

When McParlan first appeared as a witness, the Molly Maguires hoped that his testimony would concentrate on one or two of them, and that most of them would be able to escape the attention of local law enforcement, and survive to reorganize and pursue their objectives as an organization. But McParlan had given scrupulous attention to detail in his two years of undercover work, and the content of his testimony excluded no one. In all, a total of twenty members of the Molly Maguires were found guilty and hanged: ten on June 21, 1877 and ten the following year.

QUESTIONS

1. Does the labor-management strife in this case justify or tend to excuse the criminal activities of the Molly Maguires?
2. Were the Pinkertons, in their role in this case, representative of community police services?
3. On the issue of whether the use of an undercover "police" agent was an undesirable technique under the circumstances of this case, can McParlan's assignment and actions be justified?

SUMMARY

In the *McCray* case, the use of an informant was justified as being in the public interest, and the Court decided that the police did not have to disclose the informant's identity to afford the defendant a fair trial. The case in which forty-seven "lids" of marijuana were seized and the possessor of the drugs claimed exoneration because of his role as a police informer, raises the issue of whether secret sources of information may lack a vital integrity and trustworthiness. The case of the Molly Maguires and the Pinkertons reveals court approval of the work of an undercover agent—but the circumstances of the case suggest that a private police agent in the employ of "management" may not be the most reliable source of data about criminal activities connected with a bitter labor-management dispute.

At the end of each case, the questions probe the issue which is the major theme of this chapter: Is the use of informants and undercover agents a desirable police technique? This theme can also be discussed from another frame of reference, that is, whether the use of secret informers is *per se* unconstitutional, as violative of the Fourth, Fifth, and Sixth Amendments' guarantees of privacy, protection against self-incrimination, and the right to counsel.

CHAPTER FIVE

Dishonesty and Corruption

There is a rich history of dishonest employees in the police role, but there is also an increasing incidence of dishonest employees in the areas of corrections and prosecution, and—now and then—there are reports of judicial corruption or conflict of interest. But the methodology of corruption among agents of justice and the "reasonable consideration" or thing of value, which turns a previously honest person to dishonesty, have not been fully identified.

Some thing or person in the professional environment of criminal justice may contribute to dishonesty and corruption. Since the work of any agent of criminal justice involves frequent contacts with criminals and criminal schemes, there is always a clear and present moral danger in this type of employment.

Dishonesty and corruption among the nation's police is infrequent when the great number of police are considered, but police scandals recur with sufficient frequency to affect the social status of police generally.[1] Despite this damage to a major occupation in law enforcement, suggestions for innovative remedial action are usually ignored and the current rate of police dishonesty is generally accepted as an unchangeable fact of life.[2]

The concept that dishonest employees are the products of forces that are inherent to the environment of law enforcement is involved in each of the three cases in this chapter.

In Case Study 12, which is about dishonesty and corruption in the po-

[1]Arthur Neiderhoffer, *Behind the Shield* (New York: Anchor Books, 1969), p. 21.

[2]*New York Times*, 24, 25 and 26 April 1970.

lice services, there is strong evidence of this environmental influence. In the second case, Case Study 13, a story of the corruption of a correctional officer, there is also support for the concept that dishonesty is environmentally based. This is suggested because of the numerous contacts between prison staff personnel and the inmates, but one also considers that the inmate who corrupted the guard in this case may have characteristics uncommon to all of the inmates. In the case concluding the chapter, Case Study 14, there is only an inference that the environment of a prosecutor's office may develop a tolerance to dishonesty and corruption, which might lead to the acceptance of bribes when offered.

Together, these case studies present three situations for analysis and discussion in which previously honest employees of criminal justice agencies are accused of dishonesty and corruption.

The Special Crime Squad

The scene and the characters in this case are the standard ones in American criminal trials. The scene is a courtroom, and the participants are judge and jury; prosecutor and defense counsel; prosecution witness and defendant. The unusual nature of this case however, is that both the witness and the defendant are policemen.

The testimony reported here details the essential elements of the process of the corruption of a police officer. The crime charged is unstated, and the defendant is identified only as "Bob," but it is apparent that the witness being questioned is a policeman exposing police dishonesty and corruption. The testimony presents a very unpleasant picture: the corruption of almost an entire police unit. This is a unit known as "The Organized Crime Suppression Squad," or "OCSS," which is staffed with two lieutenants and fifteen detectives who specialized—at least that was their assigned function—in developing intelligence about organized crime.

CAST OF CHARACTERS

Judge	ANONYMOUS
Defense Counsel	ANONYMOUS
Assistant District Attorney	ANONYMOUS
Defendant	BOB (not otherwise identified)
Prosecution Witness	DETECTIVE SERGEANT DANIEL COSTELLO of THE SPECIAL CRIME SQUAD

SCENE 1: *A courtroom. There is a high judicial bench, an adjacent witness stand and chair, and a table and two chairs in front of the bench*

and witness stand. As the scene opens, the judge is seated on the bench, the two chairs are occupied by the defendant and his counsel, the witness chair is empty, and the Assistant District Attorney is standing in front of it.

ASSISTANT DISTRICT ATTORNEY: I would like to call my first witness: Detective Sergeant Daniel Costello. (*Sergeant Costello appears, and sits down in witness chair.*)

JUDGE: Have you been sworn in?

DETECTIVE COSTELLO: Yes, your Honor.

(*Assistant District Attorney walks toward witness stand and begins questioning Detective Costello*)

ASSISTANT DISTRICT ATTORNEY: What is your name and occupation?

DETECTIVE COSTELLO: Daniel Costello—I am a sergeant of detectives— all detectives are sergeants—and I work for the police force of this city.

ASSISTANT DISTRICT ATTORNEY: How long have you been in this occupation and rank?

DETECTIVE COSTELLO: Ten years in the police department, four years in the rank.

ASSISTANT DISTRICT ATTORNEY: About two years ago, I understand you were assigned to this new unit, the Organized Crime Suppression Squad, and that within a few days of working in your new job you visited a high official of your police force. Do you recall this event?

DETECTIVE COSTELLO: Yes, I do.

ASSISTANT DISTRICT ATTORNEY: When was it and who was involved?

DETECTIVE COSTELLO: It was just after St. Patrick's Day, March 18th, of this year. It was about ten in the morning, and the person involved was Captain Richard Jones of the Police Academy.

ASSISTANT DISTRICT ATTORNEY: Tell us in your own words what happened on this occasion.

DETECTIVE COSTELLO: I knew Captain Jones from the Academy—he was my instructor. He was a lieutenant, and I was a recruit. I told him I thought the OCSS, the whole group, was infiltrated or penetrated by the mob, the hoodlums, and narco pushers. He listened—I talked. His advice was to take it up with higher authorities in the department. He made a phone call arranging a meeting for me, and I thanked him, and left the office.

ASSISTANT DISTRICT ATTORNEY: What happened next in direct relation to this talk?

DETECTIVE COSTELLO: I met a captain from the Internal Security Division that night, at a few minutes after ten, in the parking lot of the golf course—the city one.

ASSISTANT DISTRICT ATTORNEY: Would you please identify this man and tell us, again in your own words, what happened at this meeting.

DETECTIVE COSTELLO: His name is Captain John Behan—he works directly under the chief. He came over to my car, and I told him substantially what I had told Captain Jones. He told me that I had no specific evidence that he could use, but that if I was willing to work with him, I could get the evidence. Captain Behan gave me his home phone number, and told me to call him. He said we would meet again where we were, in the golf course parking lot. That was for when I had something to tell him. We shook hands and split.

ASSISTANT DISTRICT ATTORNEY: Did you meet the captain again in this golf course parking lot? That is, Captain Behan?

DETECTIVE COSTELLO: Yes, I did. All told, I met with him about seven or eight times.

ASSISTANT DISTRICT ATTORNEY: At any of these meetings did Captain Behan spell out in any way what your job was in this new arrangement with him?

DETECTIVE COSTELLO: Yes, he did. Thoroughly. I was to work undercover, for him and the chief. I was to act as if nothing was out of order, and to come up with some specific evidence of what I had said about dishonesty.

ASSISTANT DISTRICT ATTORNEY: In this new role, did you know the defendant?

DETECTIVE COSTELLO: Yes, he was one of my associates, another detective sergeant—a member of OCSS.

ASSISTANT DISTRICT ATTORNEY: During this time of your association with the defendant, did you at any time participate with the defendant in any event which led you to make a report about him to Captain Behan?

DETECTIVE COSTELLO: Yes, and it was on the Monday after I first met Captain Behan. That would be March 21st, of this year.

ASSISTANT DISTRICT ATTORNEY: Tell us, in your own words, what happened at this time—on this occasion.

DETECTIVE COSTELLO: I met the defendant, Bob, in the Nitro Bar and Grill, on Seventh and Main Streets. It was about 11:00 A.M. He had a hoodlum with him that I knew as Big Bart, Bart Nino, and he introduced us. Nino took some money from his pocket right away and handed some bills to me. I said, "What's that for?" Nino said, "Get yourself a hat." I said, "I don't wear a hat," and gave him back the money.

ASSISTANT DISTRICT ATTORNEY: Do you know the amount of money?

DETECTIVE COSTELLO: No, I don't. Several bills, folded up. No, I do not.

ASSISTANT DISTRICT ATTORNEY: What happened next?

DETECTIVE COSTELLO: Nino shrugged his shoulders and gave the money to Bob—the defendant. Then, Nino talked a little bit about nothing much, ball games and girls, and he left. I asked Bob, "What's he buying?" He said, "Not much." Then I said something like, "Why me?" He said, "Why not, you don't use money?" Then he told me that Nino wanted to get some records taken out of our squad files about his brother—his younger brother. Bob said the kid was trying to go legit, and our records were bugging him in getting a job. I heard him out, then left and went back to the office.

ASSISTANT DISTRICT ATTORNEY: Did you do anything in relation to this conversation?

DETECTIVE COSTELLO: Yes, I did. I went to our files—everyone was out to lunch. I got young Nino's file folder out, looked at it, found he was wanted for suspicion of receiving stolen property and for suspicion of homicide in another case. I xeroxed the file papers, and I put the xerox copies in my desk drawer—which I locked—put the record file back in our filing cabinet, and then I went out to lunch myself.

ASSISTANT DISTRICT ATTORNEY: Now—at any future date, did you have anything to do with this record again?

DETECTIVE COSTELLO: Yes. It was the following Saturday, that's March 26th, this year. I went into the office early, went to our files and looked for young Nino's record. I took it out and examined it, and I found that the photo had been changed—Big Bart's photo was substituted for his brother's picture, and the wanted cards were missing.

ASSISTANT DISTRICT ATTORNEY: I show you folder marked "Nino, Alberto," and I ask you do you recognize it?

DETECTIVE COSTELLO: (*Reading*) Yes, it's the fixed-up, tampered-with folder.

ASSISTANT DISTRICT ATTORNEY: In relation to this xerox copy of the original folder in your squad files about this young Nino—what happened to that?

DETECTIVE COSTELLO: I have that here (*showing file folder*) with me now.

ASSISTANT DISTRICT ATTORNEY: Your Honor, can I have both these files marked for identification? Thank you. Your witness (*to defense counsel*), counselor.

(*Defense Counsel stands, and begins cross-examination.*)

DEFENSE COUNSEL: Are most of your fellow policemen honest?

DETECTIVE COSTELLO: Yes, most of them are honest—and hard working.

DEFENSE COUNSEL: How many policemen, in your knowledge, entered the police department for the purpose of becoming dishonest?

DETECTIVE COSTELLO: None, to my knowledge—not to my knowledge.

DEFENSE COUNSEL: I gather, from your prompt answers, that you know a great deal about your fellow policemen, is that true?

DETECTIVE COSTELLO: Well—I guess I do. They're my co-workers. Why not?

DEFENSE COUNSEL: Now—Tell the court if any conduct of yours has bothered or upset your fellow co-workers.

DETECTIVE COSTELLO: I don't— I don't understand the question.

DEFENSE COUNSEL: It's a simple question, but let me withdraw it, and phrase it in this fashion: To your knowledge has any of your conduct upset your fellow policemen?

DETECTIVE COSTELLO: Oh sure! That's a different thing. Sure, yes.

DEFENSE COUNSEL: Tell us of such an incident that you consider important.

DETECTIVE COSTELLO: Well— When I was transferred out of uniform, from patrol to the OCSS in plainclothes, I grew a beard (*puts hand to face, indicating beard*) and wore some clothes; well— the kind of clothes I only used to wear on my day off, kind of sharp, mod, I suppose. The guys in the squad used to tell me, "What a disguise!"

DEFENSE COUNSEL: And that upset you, bothered you—emotionally disturbed you?

DETECTIVE COSTELLO: Well, I don't know all that. You asked the question. Say it bugged me a bit.

DEFENSE COUNSEL: Why? Why would this remark bother you—this "Quite a disguise"?

DETECTIVE COSTELLO: It wasn't any make up, really a disguise. It was just the clothes I liked. That's why it bothered me.

DEFENSE COUNSEL: Oh, I'm beginning to understand. Now— Tell me this: in relation to the charges of dishonesty against my client, your fellow policeman, did you ever get any feedback from him about yourself as a person, or as a policeman?

DETECTIVE COSTELLO: Yes, a few times, mostly about—or along the lines of—something like: "Why don't you go along with the guys?" or, "Why do you have to be different?"

DEFENSE COUNSEL: This was in relation to your manner of dress, your appearance?

DETECTIVE COSTELLO: No, it wasn't. It was in relation to the money he was making, and that I didn't want to take—like from Nino.

DEFENSE COUNSEL: Your Honor, would you direct the witness just to answer the question.

JUDGE: No, I don't think I will. You asked the question, and it was open-ended. Let it stand along with its answer.

DEFENSE COUNSEL: Thank you, your Honor.

DEFENSE COUNSEL: Did the defendant or any of your co-workers in this Organized Crime Squad ever actually do anything to indicate any dislike for you?

DETECTIVE COSTELLO: They— They sure did. All of them did. They stopped talking to me. Except when they had to, like a phone call for me, then it was a "Here, you—" Real brief. And they would stop talking to one another when I came in the room, or walked up to them on the street.

DEFENSE COUNSEL: This animosity resulted from your dirty work, the role of informer, or spying on your fellow workers?

DETECTIVE COSTELLO: No, Counselor. At that time, no one knew of what you term "dirty work." All they knew was that I wouldn't do any business with the hoodlums—that I wanted to do my job just like I get paid for it.

DEFENSE COUNSEL: There is entrapment in your role, is there not?

ASSISTANT DISTRICT ATTORNEY: Your Honor, I object. The question—

JUDGE: (*Interrupting*) Sustained.

DEFENSE COUNSEL: (*Resuming questioning*) Since you place such a premium on doing what you get paid for, did you ever counsel or advise my client to do the same thing?

DETECTIVE COSTELLO: You sure you want to hear this?

DEFENSE COUNSEL: I asked the question.

DETECTIVE COSTELLO: Just before I left the Nitro bar on the day we met Big Bart Nino, I said to Bob, the defendant: "My God, you're making ten thousand dollars a year. You could never make this kind of money on the outside doing any other kind of work. You know you have a family, kids. Don't be stupid. Think about it." That was how it ended.

DEFENSE COUNSEL: Was there any response to these words of yours— any words said at all by my client?

DETECTIVE COSTELLO: No, not much. Something like, "If I really did, think about it— I'd blow my brains out."

QUESTIONS

1. Do the facts of this case justify a conclusion that police dishonesty is an inescapable part of the "system"?

2. Is the "thing of value" in this attempt to corrupt Detective Costello the money which would be given to him, or the approval of his associates?

3. If you were a member of the jury in this case, would you consider Detective Costello to be a credible witness, and his testimony truthful?

The Prison "Mule"

The idea for this case study originated in a two-part story in a West Coast newspaper, under the headline: "How I Made My Mule." The author was an inmate of a nearby state prison, who had just been convicted on a charge of possessing illegal drugs for the purpose of sale. In an editor's note accompanying the first installment of this story, the author was introduced as the leader of a drug-selling ring at the state prison. The case story is told simply. One of the two characters plays the role of listener, while the process of corruption is unfolded by the inmate who made George Wilson (a correctional officer, or guard) his "mule."

CAST OF CHARACTERS

State Prison Inmate	LADISLAUS FARGO
District Attorney's Investigator	JAMES DOUGLAS
State Prison Employee	GEORGE WILSON

SCENE 1: *Conference room in a state prison. There are bars on the window. The room is without pictures and it is furnished with a heavy wooden table and several chairs. The time is a few weeks after George Wilson, a prison employee, was caught smuggling unlawful drugs into the prison for sale to inmates. Wilson and several inmates have been indicted and are awaiting trial.*

INMATE: Your boss got my letter without any trouble, eh. They call me Lad around here.

INVESTIGATOR: Yeah, he did. He didn't like to get it as a "kite"—but I guess the fact that you could smuggle a letter out of prison did impress him. He told me to hop right up here. Call me Jim.

INMATE: Jim, like I wrote in my letter, this is a bum rap for old George; and if I had written through regular prison channels that I could cop a plea for old George Wilson the administration upstairs would have flipped. To them, upstairs here, he's the worst: a dishonest officer—a guard who took money from an inmate to bring drugs—and H, heroin at that—into the institution. They don't want to hear anything about helping old George; all they want to hear is five-to-life for him. And he'd die in prison. An ex-officer can't serve time in prison.

INVESTIGATOR: Okay. Maybe it makes sense. I don't know how you can help Wilson. I looked the case over before I left the office, they have him good.

INMATE: Let me talk for a little while, I'll show you. This is a thing that we can really do with anybody. That's what I put in the letter to your boss. Old George didn't become a mule; we made him—I made him. It could have been any one of a half dozen other officers. He didn't have any real criminal intent. He's the victim. That's the thing I think hooked your boss—that Old George was the victim of a crime, not a participant —not one of us. We—I—robbed him of his job and his good name. Don't that make him a victim?

INVESTIGATOR: Whoaaa— (*taking out small notebook*) Let's start at the beginning. Me— I don't buy this victim bit. Wilson took your money to smuggle drugs in to the prison. That's a violation of law. He's a crook, just like—

INMATE: (*Interrupting*) Like me, that's what you mean to say. Go ahead, say it; but it isn't true. George was a victim.

INVESTIGATOR: Free personnel aren't supposed to get involved with inmates. Years ago, they wouldn't even—or weren't really allowed—to talk to you.

INMATE: I'll start at the beginning. You pick your mule from any one of five or six officers who are giving off signs. What kinds of signs? Signs of unhappiness with their job, the shift boss, the head screw, their wife, mother-in-law, regulations, the Highway Patrol—anything. They bitch about something. It's a sign in big letters.

INVESTIGATOR: (*Writing in notebook*) You mean a sour guy, a guy maybe ready to strike back at the world—things going wrong for him?

INMATE: You don't walk up to an officer and ask him to bring "H" into prison for you. You see a guy give off these signs, then you try to recognize the mood and play to it. You're sympathetic about whatever he's bitching about. Then you bitch a tiny bit about something in line with what he's crying about, and he'll sympathize some with you—not much, but this is the beginning, see—

INVESTIGATOR: I see— How often do you do this?

INMATE: How often? That's a laugh. You forget we got a lot of time in here. I saw old George every day he worked, five days a week, and for eight hours a day. After some of these daily contacts for a couple of weeks, I'd test. I'd avoid George, wouldn't talk to him. Sure enough, he would stop me and say: "What's up? What's up your snoot?" I'd deny it. "Who me?" I'd say nothing was wrong. I would say I was a little bugged maybe, but that I'd get over it. You see? He was testing friendship; I was testing the development of my mule.

INVESTIGATOR: I'm beginning to see. When your prospective smuggler passed these tests, then what?

INMATE: You start small. Some unimportant item to go out, or come in. It doesn't matter what. I started mine with a "kite"—a letter to be smuggled out of the institution. I know another guy started his mule with a magazine, coming into the institution. I asked old George, "Do me a favor. Mail a letter for me. "Look," and I showed him the flap on the envelope was open, "you can read it yourself—it's harmless." He wouldn't touch it; but he didn't say he'd write up a beef on me for trying to get a kite out. He said, "If it's so harmless, mail it upstairs." I said, "Look, it is harmless, but I don't want it to go through upstairs. It's personal and the gal I'm writing to is a con's wife, and I don't want it to get back to him through the administration." George took the letter. He grumbled something about it better be harmless, but he took it and mailed it for me on the outside.

INVESTIGATOR: What if he had written you up? That would have hurt you and your privileges?

INMATE: Mostly, if you guessed wrong on a guy, they just say no. Some, and I wouldn't go to bat for this kind of guy like I am trying to help old George, they would say: "What's in it for me?" I don't like that kind of guy. He's going to end up getting caught, doing too much smuggling, and then he involves you.

INVESTIGATOR: I can see that. He's the business man then, not you. Did you pay Wilson?

INMATE: Yes, I gave him five bucks for the letter. I insisted. He didn't want to take it at first. You know an officer don't make much, and a five or ten-dollar bill is a lot to him. Believe me, a fiver for a harmless letter looks big.

INVESTIGATOR: What did you do next? Another letter?

INMATE: No, I asked him to bring me in some chewing gum. It's not sold in here, and it's a luxury. No trouble—he delivered it the next day.

I told him these were goodies that I could get a deuce a pack for, and that I'd split with him. This time I gave him ten bucks, and he bought the gum, fifty cents worth, out of his own pocket.

INVESTIGATOR: Now you had him? Is that it?

INMATE: Yeah, that's step two. It's still quite harmless stuff, but he did take money. I had him, but not quite up to step-three level. I went to work on him by saying: "George, you like gals besides your wife, but that takes dough—and you're not getting any younger. How about making a C-note, one hundred American dollars, real money?" "You trying to get me in trouble?" he said. I told him, "George, I'm not talking about a pistol, and I'm not going to make a bomb. It's only some more goodies, but this time it's stuff that makes it easier to serve time. I guarantee it won't be anything that could hurt another officer."

INVESTIGATOR: Do you think he knew it was narcotics—heroin? He must have known.

INMATE: No, no! All he knew was that it was not a gun or anything to make a bomb out of.

INVESTIGATOR: Did anything else happen before he brought the heroin in for you and got caught?

INMATE: No. It took us about a month to make the outside arrangements to get an ounce of heroin. Then I gave old George six hundred dollars. I told him to keep a hundred dollars, and pay the other five bills to the guy that would bring the stuff to him. We set it up for the stuff to be delivered to George at a bar in his home neighborhood that he visited every day.

INVESTIGATOR: How did he get caught?

INMATE: Let me finish. Next day, I went to the key locker—I clean cells, you know—to get some keys and there was the package. Old George had brought it in. It was small. George hadn't tampered with the package. Now that's step three. I had him hooked. My mule was made. He had taken a C-note and brought in real felony contraband. Now, he not only risked losing his job, but he risked going to jail. At this stage, you can ask your mule to do anything. He can't turn you down. This is how—not me—but how others get guns into these joints.

INVESTIGATOR: He—your mule—is at your mercy at this stage, and from there on in. That's for sure. Is there any variation on this?

INMATE: No, maybe— If you need another officer real bad, a hurry-up mule, then you go to work on your own mule to hook the guy. That's about the only variation. Except, don't let your mule get caught—that hurts.

INVESTIGATOR: You don't like your mule to be discovered— I can see that.

INMATE: That's my plug for George. Do you think it will help him?

INVESTIGATOR: (*Rising and extending his hand*) I don't know, but I'll shake hands on my promise to put this story on paper, and put it on the District Attorney's desk.

INMATE: That's good enough for me.

INVESTIGATOR: (*To offstage*) We're through in here.

QUESTIONS

1. Do the facts of this case justify the conclusion that dishonesty in a state prison is institutionalized (an inescapable part of the "system")?

2. Is the "thing of value" in this process of corrupting George Wilson the money given to him by inmate Fargo or the friendship of this inmate?

3. If you were the District Attorney in this case would you consider this story to be truthful?

The Prosecutor as Accused

This case study asks if there might be a special ethic among attorneys who serve as prosecutors. In theory, the many contacts that prosecutors have with criminals might develop a tolerance for the criminal behavior that they experience so regularly in their daily work. Also, the regular participation in "bargaining" sessions that prosecutors conduct to attempt to secure guilty pleas from defendants, in order to keep court dockets reasonably clear[3] may tend to lower a prosecutor's threshold for dishonesty.

John J. Farrell was a young attorney who graduated from law school with honors, but without the money or friends necessary to establish himself in private practice. He pyramided a friendship with one of his law-school professors into a minor post with the Eisenhower administration's Department of Justice in Washington, D.C. Impatient with the next-in-line promotion policy of the national Republican party, Farrell, next, offered his legal talents to a former associate in the Department of Justice—a man who had patiently waited his turn politically, and was now being appointed as a Federal Prosecutor in his home town, a large Eastern city. Since the new prosecutor asked for the resignations of the staff of his predecessor (appointed during the Truman administration), John Farrell was appointed to the now vacant position of assistant prosecutor in the office of the federal district attorney for the United States District in which "X" City was located.

---

[3]Donald J. Newman, "Pleading Guilty for Considerations: A Study of Bargain Justice," in *Readings in Criminal Justice*, ed. Jack Ronald Foster (Berkeley, Calif.: McCutchan, 1969), pp. 269–78.

"X" City has a population of over a million persons; dominates the surrounding metropolitan area; and, because of its location in the mainstream of Eastern urban centers, it has its local *cosa nostra* "family," and an above-average crime rate.

Traditionally, a local U.S. Attorney's office is headed by a lawyer who is next in line for a judicial appointment. This does not necessarily mean that the judgeship appointment is guaranteed, but it does mean that it is in the offing. No such implied political promise, however, is understood or made to the assistant U.S. attorneys. The opportunity offered to an ambitious person willing to work in such a post is nothing more than an opportunity for self-improvement: work in and out of court as a prosecutor and a chance to learn the trade of a trial attorney. It is a nebulous arrangement, one in which the young lawyer's future lies in the contacts made in the job, instead of in direct advancement. Consequently, the position of assistant U.S. attorney is known politically as an "up-and-out" post.

John Farrell was exposed to a conditioning process as a young federal prosecutor. He quickly learned the rationale for the past actions of his predecessor's assistants; the ongoing conduct of other cases by his present associates; and the rewards of his office in the past and the present. Unlike the state courts, the federal courts do not process any great number of simple crimes emanating from anger or need, such as murder and burglary. Therefore, John Farrell was also conditioned by his contacts with offenders against United States laws. Thus, he encountered many criminals in the illicit traffic in narcotics, men who were members of the national crime syndicate; and he also met tax-fraud offenders, individuals also connected in some fashion with the cosa nostra and its operation.

Farrell soon learned the so-called art of plea negotiation, and the methods of preparing cases for trial. He learned to bully defendants and their counsel into pleas of guilty, in exchange for agreements to prosecute on a lesser charge, or to only pursue one count of a six- or seven-count indictment. He became skilled in trading one crime partner against another when he found group loyalty to be weak, working the "better-him-than-you" theme to develop a witness who would appear in court and testify against his criminal associates, thus giving Farrell an open-and-shut case leading to a speedy conviction.

John Farrell, over a period of years, became a senior prosecutor in his federal district. And, naturally, he became a friend of many prominent persons in "X" City, and a person cultivated by others for his own friendship. Farrell was on the way up. He was active in Republican politics; served on several important associations and committees; and he appeared to prosper financially. No doubt, he would step "up-and-out" to a lucrative private law practice, or to a better-paying position in the federal legal complex in Washington.

Now, it came to pass, as a bitter cup for all Republican office-holders, that Eisenhower and his administration left Washington, and the Democratic administration of John F. Kennedy moved into the nation's capital. In the usual course of events, a new federal prosecutor was appointed in "X" City. The new appointee terminated the appointment of several assistant prosecutors, including that of John Farrell.

Farrell did very well in the private law practice in "X" City which he next took up. Unfortunately, most of his clients appeared to come to him through friendships made while Farrell was a federal prosecutor. Thus, the police of a nearby city reported to their state boxing commission that Farrell's picture was in their possession, and that it showed him to be present at a dinner party in honor of two top hoodlums who were known to be national controllers of the cosa nostra fight "rackets." And a federal narcotics agent reported to the police of "X" City that John Farrell had flown in and out of Las Vegas on weekend trips no less than ten times in the last three months.

Information about these activities didn't reach the news media; therefore, the announcement of Farrell's indictment as a "fixer" received considerable publicity. He was charged with perjury and obstruction of justice. The new assistant federal attorney who was prosecuting the case against Farrell said that he had four witnesses who would testify to Farrell's guilty conduct while serving as an assistant U.S. prosecutor.

As the case developed, two of the witnesses had prior convictions for tax fraud. They had arranged "deals" for lesser sentences and immunity with the Kennedy-generation prosecutor, in exchange for their cooperation in exposing the graft and corruption of the Eisenhower-generation's John Farrell. The two other witnesses were found to have extensive criminal records linking them to operations identified with the crime syndicate.

The prosecution's case against Farrell alleged that there was a criminal conspiracy in which Farrell was paid $50,000 in cash to persuade another federal prosecutor to drop charges against two underworld figures who were about to be included in a pending indictment in a tax-fraud case. In support of this accusation, there was testimony in which the prosecution witnesses stated the facts of the cash payment, and described a meeting that they had with the prosecutor preparing the indictment.

This alleged ally of Farrell in corrupting justice, the other former prosecutor, took the stand as a defense witness and denied any such meeting or any payment from Farrell, stating that he had "waived" the indictment against the two witnesses on his own initiative, and as part of a justifiable legal strategy to successfully prosecute second-level offenders in the case.

The defense rested its case without allowing the defendant to take the stand in his own defense or to deny the payment of $50,000, his presence at the alleged meeting, and any action to persuade an associate to "waive" anything.

In the prosecution summary, the prosecutor asked the jury to view the witnesses not as criminals unworthy of belief, but as underworld businessmen testifying about a business transaction. The defense theme, in its end-of-trial summary, was one of moral indignation and outrage at the embarrassment that such charges brought to the defendant and his alleged accomplice in the U.S. attorney's office.

The trial judge was very unsympathetic to the defendant in his instructions to the jury. However, in less than a day, the jury returned to court and reported a total inability to arrive at a verdict. The trial judge polled the jurors, thanked them, and concluded the case.

The prosecutor stated he would retry the case, but months passed without action. Finally, in a little-noticed court action, Farrell's attorney succeeded in having the case dismissed because of the prosecutor's failure to move for a speedy trial.

QUESTIONS

1. Do the facts of this case study justify the conclusion that dishonesty among prosecutors is institutionalized (an inescapable part of the system)?
2. Is the "thing of value" in this case more likely to be the money allegedly paid to Farrell or the approval and friendship of the prosecutor involved or the person or persons offering the bribe?
3. On the facts of this case study, is there sufficient legally significant evidence to justify the retrial of John Farrell?

SUMMARY

There is a need for understanding the processes of corruption in law enforcement and criminal justice. Police units, correctional institutions, and courts share the goals of properly administrating justice, and any dishonesty or corruption threatens the achievement of this objective. Additionally, if it is true that the environment of employment in these agencies is instrumental in fostering dishonesty and corruption, there is a great need for research which will chart appropriate remedial action to keep the honest persons who enter these occupations from becoming dishonest.

While each of the three cases in this chapter present the unique problems of corruption in different areas of law enforcement (police, corrections, and public prosecutors), the three cases taken as a whole, offer an opportunity to analyze, evaluate, and discuss the issue of institutionalization as a factor in dishonesty and corruption in law enforcement and criminal justice. It was for this reason that the questions at the end of each case are similar—inquiring into the same areas of dishonesty as a function of institutionalization.

CHAPTER SIX

On the Issue of Guilt
or Innocence

One of the most basic safeguards in the administration of justice in America is the presumption of innocence, even when a person is accused of crime. Unfortunately, practitioners in criminal justice tend to view this requirement of presuming a person's innocence as a legal fiction whose role is solely to determine the order of accepting evidence in a criminal proceeding, and as a convenient starting place to begin determining guilt beyond a reasonable doubt.

Additionally, the people in most American communities reinforce this professional frame of reference by a like belief in the guilt of persons indicted, arrested, or charged with crime. It is not so much a rejection of the basic presumption of innocence by the people of the community as it is a subliminal acceptance of the validity of the police and prosecutor's judgment that the person accused of crime is, in fact, guilty.

Any deviation from the basic presumption of innocence seriously threatens the integrity of a criminal trial as a proceeding in which fair treatment is accorded all the parties, and in which guilt must be proved beyond a reasonable doubt. When a man is judged unfairly and adjudged guilty of a crime despite his innocence, there is a triple injustice: the innocent accused is not given a fair trial; he loses his physical freedom by going to prison; and the guilty person will escape justice.

The two cases in this chapter, Case Studies 15 and 16, have an amazing similarity. They deal with two different arrests for the same crime; a double homicide of two young women in New York City. The prime issue in both cases is whether the defendants, who were each in their turn accused of the crime, were guilty or innocent.[1] Also important are the circumstances which contributed to an innocent person's trial in the first case, and the circumstances which threatened a fair trial for the man in the second case.[2] In the first case, a man named Whitmore was arrested, indicted, and then exonerated. In the second case, a man named Robles was identified as the person who really committed the double murder of the two young women.

[1]Bernard Lefkowitz and Kenneth G. Gross, *The Victims: The Wylie-Hoffert Murder Case—and Its Strange Aftermath* (New York: Putnam's, 1969), pp. 13–43.
[2]Selwyn Raab, *Justice in the Back Room* (New York: World Publishing, 1967), pp. 1–5, 9–15.

Wylie, Hoffert, and Whitmore

This case involves a double murder and a lengthy investigation in which George Whitmore, Jr., is arrested and charged with the crime.[3] For clarity, the case is presented in the form of a chronology, beginning with the day of the crime.

WEDNESDAY, AUGUST 28, 1963—
THE DAY OF THE CRIME

Janice Wylie, twenty-one, and Emily Hoffert, twenty-three, were found bound and stabbed to death in Apartment 3-C at 57 East 88th Street, New York City. Their bodies were found by Max Wylie, father of Miss Wylie, and by Patricia Tolles, a roommate who shared the murder-scene apartment with the two victims.

Miss Tolles, who had last seen the victims when she left for work at 9:30 that morning, returned from work at 6:40 P.M., and found the apartment in disarray. Shocked and upset, she did not go through the apartment, although she did glance into the bathroom. She called Max Wiley from the telephone in the foyer of the apartment, and he came directly over from his home a few blocks away. They examined the apartment and found the bodies of the two victims in a bedroom, between a wall and a bed. Miss Wylie was nude, Miss Hoffert was fully clothed. Two knives were on a

---

[3]Fred Shapiro, *Whitmore* (Indianapolis and New York: Bobbs-Merrill, 1969), pp. 75–7.

FIGURE 7   Janice Wylie (left) and Emily Hoffert were murdered in their New York City apartment.

radiator cover near the bodies, and there was another knife on the basin in the bathroom of the apartment which was opposite the crime-scene bedroom. The wrists and ankles of both victims were tied, and their bodies were bound together at the wrists and waists. Cloth strips, torn or cut from a bedsheet and a bedspread, were used for this restraint. There was no blood in any room other than the bedroom in which the victims were found. The drawers of dressers and cabinets were open, and their contents were dumped on the floor, on beds, and on dresser tops. Miss Tolles said that nothing was missing, and that neither the victims, nor she herself, possessed any valuable jewelry or large sums of cash. Preliminary police investigation revealed no sign of forced entry, and no witness who had seen or heard anything suspicious was found. Chief Medical Examiner, Dr. Michael Halpern, said the bodies of the victims had been mutilated viciously, but there was no apparent evidence of sexual assault.

THURSDAY, AUGUST 29, 1963—
1 DAY AFTER THE CRIME

A search of the apartment by police identification technicians revealed numerous fingerprints. All such traces were collected and then processed by the police. The two knives found in the crime-scene bedroom had broken blades, but the complete blades were recovered from the floor nearby. The knife found in the bathroom was intact, and identified as a standard pointed steak knife. The origin of knives was apparently the kitchen of the apartment.

Continued questioning of neighbors and building employees failed to locate anyone who had seen or heard anything suspicious or directly related to the crime apartment. One neighbor reported meeting a stranger in the elevator, who he described as of medium build and "baby-faced."

Chief Medical Examiner Halpern said, in a preliminary autopsy report, that the cause of death for both victims was multiple stab wounds in the neck, chest, and abdomen, and that Miss Hoffert had head wounds in which glass was found, indicating blows by a weapon such as a soft-drink bottle. An electric night-table clock was found near the bodies. Its plug was out of the wall and on the floor a few feet from a wall outlet, and a good portion of its electric cord was partially under the torso of victim Wylie. The time on the stopped clock was 10:35.

Max Wylie stated that his daughter Janice had received a threatening phone call on or about August 18, and that she was terrified by it. The caller left a name, Joe Hunter, and a telephone number, Wylie added, but

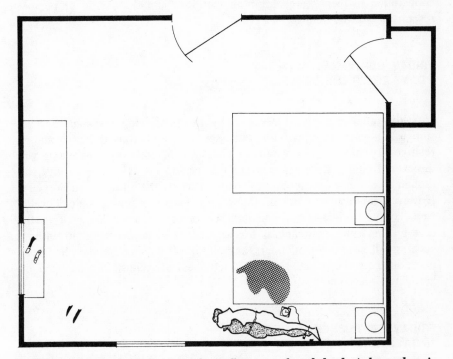

FIGURE 8   Janice Wylie and Emily Hoffert were found dead, tied together, in one of the bedrooms of their two-bedroom apartment. Key items of evidence were a massive blood stain on one of the beds, two broken bloody knives (the blades were found on the floor, the handles on a radiator cover), and an electric clock found near the bodies of the two victims.

when his daughter called the number a woman who identified herself as the subscriber for that telephone number said she knew of no man named Hunter or any similar name.

FRIDAY, AUGUST 30, 1963—
2 DAYS AFTER THE CRIME

Newsweek, where Miss Wylie had worked, offered a ten-thousand-dollar reward for information leading to the arrest and conviction of the murderer or murderers. Continuing investigation revealed that Miss Hoffert had left the apartment shortly after her roommate, Patricia Tolles, left for work at 9:30 A.M. The victim then drove north to Riverdale to return a borrowed car and pick up her own automobile. She was placed in the Riverdale area up until 11 A.M., through contacts with friends and the garage proprietor. The time span of the crime could now be set between 9:30 A.M. and 6:40 P.M. for victim Wylie; and 11:30 A.M. to 6:40 P.M. for victim Hoffert. Police established a public information telephone number, and asked for public cooperation in their search for both witnesses and the person or persons responsible for the killings.

FRIDAY, SEPTEMBER 6, 1963—
9 DAYS AFTER THE CRIME

No substantial clues were revealed by the continuing investigation, despite a far-reaching search for witnesses, and numerous inquiries among relatives, friends, and associates of victims. No motive for the crime was discovered either. Burglary was not believed to be the actual motive, although an attempt was apparently made to create the illusion of a burglary. However, no cash was stolen, and several pieces of jewelry and a watch were left untouched. Over one hundred detectives were assigned to the case by this time. The canvass for witnesses had been concluded without success. All known sex offenders, and all known daytime burglars had been questioned by the police, and their activities on August 28 had been investigated—all to no avail.

FRIDAY, SEPTEMBER 13, 1963—
16 DAYS AFTER THE CRIME

The report of the fingerprint search and processing revealed that no fingerprints were present on the suspect murder weapons (3 knives), and that a total of nine partial sets of fingerprints were found in the apartment. Seven of these sets corresponded with those of the victims, relatives, friends, or occupants of apartment. The two remaining sets of partial fingerprints did not have sufficient characteristics for overt identification by any search of criminal justice files; but they were marked for possible use as suspects were developed through other information and evidence in the case.

SEPTEMBER 27, 1963—
33 DAYS AFTER THE CRIME

In the continuing investigation of the Wylie-Hoffert murders, detectives had interviewed over five hundred persons, but to date no identity of the murderer or murderers had been revealed, nor had any witness been found who observed anyone leaving the apartment or any suspicious person in the building during the time span of the crime. Investigators had been seeking someone who observed a blood-spattered person, or one carrying a bundle or bag. The police believed that the killer's clothing was splashed with blood during the crime, and he then would have had blood-stained clothing when he fled from the scene—unless he had changed clothes at the crime scene. In that case, he would have carried out his bloody garments in a bag or bundle.

THURSDAY, OCTOBER 31, 1963—
64 DAYS AFTER THE CRIME

Continuing investigation exhausted all leads contained in telephone and memorandum books of the victims, and all other memoranda such as cards and letters with names, telephone numbers or other identification that were found in the apartment. Police had also investigated all names and other leads supplied by friends and relatives of the victims, including the "Joe Hunter" lead supplied by Max Wylie. They also followed leads gathered through the over one thousand telephone calls received by the special public information number. To date, no description or other identification of the murderer or murderers, or of any suspicious person seen leaving the death-scene apartment or its vicinity on the day of the crime, had been secured. The detail of detectives, now reduced to twenty-four, had reoriented the continuing investigation to investigate (1) all previous crimes in which knives were used; (2) all persons moving out of the neighborhood; and (3) persons who left state mental-health institutions or prisons just prior to the crime, or who had been admitted or committed since the crime.

THURSDAY, FEBRUARY 27, 1964—
183 DAYS AFTER THE CRIME

Detectives assigned to the continuing investigation had now interviewed, questioned, and investigated over one thousand suspects. Most suspects had been fully exonerated. About ten of these individuals required some verification of their activities on the day of the crime. To date, no one of these persons was classed as a major suspect, and no substantial clue to the identity of the murderer or murderers had been discovered.

SATURDAY, APRIL 24, 1964—
240 DAYS AFTER THE CRIME

George Whitmore, Jr., nineteen, was arrested for the Wylie-Hoffert killings. At about 6:00 A.M., Friday, April 23, a Brooklyn police officer who was searching an area in which an assault, robbery, and attempted rape had been committed a few hours earlier, spotted a suspect and took him to the police station. The victim of the robbery and attempted rape, Mrs. Ella Borrero, was brought to the police station and identified the suspect— George Whitmore. He confessed to the crime. He was booked for the robbery and attempted rape of Mrs. Borrero. A search revealed no weapon and no drugs, but two photographs were found in his wallet. The suspect said they were "girlfriends." Further questioning led to Whitmore confessing to the murder of Mrs. Minnie Edmonds, age forty-six. Mrs. Edmonds' body had been found in a backyard at 444 Blake Avenue, Brooklyn, on April 14—ten days earlier. Death had resulted from multiple stab and slash wounds from a knife or similar weapon.

Detective Edward Bulger, who was present at the questioning of Whitmore in the Edmonds case, had been assigned to the investigation of the Wylie-Hoffert murders in its early stages. He thought the two photographs found in Whitmore's wallet resembled the blonde, blue-eyed Wylie girl and her roommate-victim. Further questioning resulted in Whitmore admitting to the murders of Misses Wylie and Hoffert. Whitmore's formal statement of guilt in the double murder was taken under the direction of Peter Koste, an assistant district attorney in the Manhattan district attorney's office.

Whitmore seemed to know details of the double homicide that had never been made public. In his statement, Whitmore gave the brand name of the broken soft-drink bottle that had been found, and he stated that he broke the blades of two of the knives used in the attack by using his heel and the floor, as in breaking a stick of wood. Lastly, he admitted that he took the photograph of Miss Wylie from the dresser of the crime-scene bedroom.

Whitmore was arraigned before Judge James J. Comerford in a Brooklyn court. An attorney, Jerome Leftow, was appointed to represent Whitmore when he stated that he was without legal counsel. After a brief out-of-court conference between Whitmore and his new attorney, both returned to court and Mr. Leftow told Judge Comerford that his client had made certain statements to the police but that they were made under duress and stress, and that his client now recants and repudiates all the confessions he had made. Whitmore was remanded to jail without bail by Judge Comerford for a hearing on the next Thursday.

TUESDAY, APRIL 27, 1964—
243 DAYS AFTER THE CRIME

Jerome Leftow now claimed that his client, George Whitmore, Jr., had asked police to give him a lie detector test when he was arrested the previous Friday. Additional data released by police connecting Whitmore to the Wylie-Hoffert murders was the substance of an unofficial statement published in the New York *Journal-American*. This press story stated that Whitmore knew the location of a razor blade found on the floor of crime-scene bedroom, knew where its wrapper had been found in the bathroom, and was able to describe a Noxzema jar left on the bloody floor, and told of blood spots that were found on the bedroom window shade.

TUESDAY, APRIL 28, 1964—
244 DAYS AFTER THE CRIME

Whitmore was indicted by the Brooklyn Grand Jury on first degree murder charges in the fatal stabbing of Mrs. Minnie Edmonds. The jury heard five witnesses: Mrs. Edmonds' husband, two detectives, a stenographer who recorded Whitmore's confession, and an assistant medical examiner.

WEDNESDAY, APRIL 29, 1964—
245 DAYS AFTER THE CRIME

Whitmore pleaded not guilty to first-degree murder in the knife slaying of Mrs. Minnie Edmonds in an arraignment for pleading. Whitmore was accompanied by his lawyer, Jerome Leftow, who repeated the earlier statements that his client's confessions were obtained by police through duress and harassment. Presiding Justice Myles F. MacDonald accepted the plea, and remanded the defendant to jail until his trial, now scheduled for June.

In Manhattan, a grand jury began to hear witnesses in the Wylie-Hoffert case. Peter Koste, assistant district attorney, questioned several witnesses. It was Mr. Koste who questioned Whitmore in a Brooklyn police station on the night of Whitmore's arrest for another crime—the Borrero rape.

WEDNESDAY, MAY 6, 1964—
253 DAYS AFTER THE CRIME

Whitmore was indicted by a Manhattan grand jury in the knife slaying of Janice Wylie and Emily Hoffert. The jury presented a two-count murder indictment to Justice Charles Marks, who ordered Whitmore taken into custody and arraigned for pleading. Whitmore pleaded "not guilty" to the murder charge.

FRIDAY, OCTOBER 17, 1964—
317 DAYS AFTER THE CRIME

Psychiatrists at Bellevue Hospital found George Whitmore, Jr., sane and able to stand trial for the Wylie-Hoffert murders. The finding concluded the longest study of any one patient in the long history of Bellevue's Psychiatric Center. Whitmore had been committed to Bellevue last May by Justice Charles Marks, following his arraignment and not-guilty plea in the Wylie-Hoffert case.

SUNDAY, NOVEMBER 1, 1964—
331 DAYS AFTER THE CRIME

New York detectives located a new suspect in the Wylie-Hoffert murders. He was not named, but was described as a twenty-two-year-old narcotics addict with a criminal history of burglary and drug abuse.

TUESDAY, NOVEMBER 11, 1964—
341 DAYS AFTER THE CRIME

The trial of George Whitmore, Jr., for the assault and attempted rape of Mrs. Ella Borrero began with a statement by Assistant District Attorney

Aaron Koota (now district attorney-elect). He said it was his decision to bring this case to trial prior to the two pending indictments for murder (Mrs. Edmonds in Brooklyn; Misses Wylie and Hoffert in Manhattan) against Whitmore.

THURSDAY, NOVEMBER 12, 1964—
342 DAYS AFTER THE CRIME

Mrs. Ella Borrero made an in-court identification of George Whitmore, Jr., as the person who assaulted and attempted to rape her last April 23. On direct examination, the twenty-one-year-old witness testified that she got off the subway at the Rockaway Avenue station at about 1:00 A.M., on her way home from her work as a nurse; that she became aware of being followed by a man before she had walked a half block; and that a block later she noticed that this man was moving closer. She said that she then left the sidewalk and began to walk down the middle of the deserted street, but in less than another half block this man caught up with her, snatched her pocketbook, and then threw one arm around her neck from the front, and the other across her mouth and held her. He warned her against screaming, saying: "If you scream, I'll kill you." She testified that he then walked her, in this face-to-face position, down the street for two blocks to a location about a half block from her home. Here, her attacker made her walk down an alleyway stairs to the basement of a building she believed to be 192 Bristol Street, and he forced her against the basement wall. In her struggles, Mrs. Borrero reported, she got her mouth clear and screamed. She then related the facts of a policeman's arrival and his rescue of her, and rose from the witness stand to make her in-court identification of Whitmore. On cross-examination, Mrs. Borrero admitted that she was not given the opportunity to pick Whitmore out of a police line-up when she made the initial police identification about thirty hours after the crime. She testified that she first identified Whitmore at her local police station house by looking through a peephole into a room in which there were two occupants— the defendant and a detective.

FRIDAY, NOVEMBER 13, 1964—
343 DAYS AFTER THE CRIME

The confession of George Whitmore, Jr. to the assault and attempted rape of Mrs. Ella Borrero was questioned by Whitmore's attorney at his Brooklyn trial. The jury was ordered out of the court room for the admissibility hearing. On direct examination, Whitmore testified that he had been beaten about the head and shoulders by detectives in the interrogation room that night until he couldn't take it anymore, and he finally nodded his head in response to questions about his guilt. On cross-examination, Whitmore admitted that he had not made a timely complaint to the district attorney who took his formal statement, or any complaint in court at the time of his arraignment on the day following the alleged beating.

The two detectives who secured the confession were also witnesses. Both men denied the use of force and stated that Whitmore had no bruises on him at the time of arraignment.

The presiding judge ruled Whitmore's confession was admissible and recalled the jury to the courtroom.

**THURSDAY, NOVEMBER 19, 1964—
349 DAYS AFTER THE CRIME**

The jury in the Brooklyn trial of George Whitmore, Jr., returned a verdict of guilty in the assault and attempted rape of Mrs. Borrero. The jury received the case at noon, and reported its verdict at 9:30 P.M. Reference to the pending murder charges against Whitmore were scrupulously avoided during the seven-day trial, and jurors received daily judicial admonitions not to read or listen to news accounts concerning any other charges against the defendant. Jerome Leftow, the defense counsel, said the most damaging evidence in the case had been the victim's in-court identification of Whitmore and Whitmore's confession.

**SATURDAY, JANUARY 2, 1965—
393 DAYS AFTER THE CRIME**

Legal counsel for George Whitmore, Jr., decided to apply to the Brooklyn courts for a reversal of his recent trial and conviction of assault and attempted rape on the grounds that Whitmore did not receive a fair trial because jurors were prejudiced by publicity regarding pending murder charges. Jerome Leftow, who was Whitmore's counsel in the Borrero case, said that the Brooklyn district attorney-elect's action in trying Whitmore on a felony less than murder was designed solely to injure Whitmore's chances of a fair trial in the pending murder indictments by labeling him as a prior felony offender.

Manhattan's district attorney, Frank S. Hogan, refused comment on the eight-month delay in the trial of Whitmore for the Wylie-Hoffert killings. Police reporters pointed to three factors that might account for the delay: (1) identity of the young blonde girl in the photograph found on Whitmore was in dispute; (2) whether the photograph was really taken from the death-scene apartment in 88th Street was also in dispute; and (3) a new suspect, a twenty-two-year-old man with a record of drug abuses and burglary, had been questioned and was under investigation.

QUESTIONS

1. On the basis of available legally significant evidence likely to be admissible in court upon trial, is further action by the prosecutor against George Whitmore, Jr., for the Wylie-Hoffert killings justified?

2. Does the role of prosecutor in making the decision to prosecute an accused involve a preliminary evaluation of evidence on the issue of guilt or innocence?

3. What evidence collected by police, other than Whitmore's confession to the double murder, supports the police theory about this crime, and the conclusion about Whitmore's guilt?

4. Do any of the facts in this case study about Whitmore's alleged crimes in Brooklyn (against Mrs. Borrero, and Mrs. Edmonds) support the police theory of his guilt in the Wylie-Hoffert murders?

Wylie, Hoffert, and Robles

Richard Robles, a twenty-two-year-old narcotics addict on parole in an aggravated assault case, was arrested on January 26, 1965, and booked at the 104th Street police station on charges of killing Janice Wylie and Emily Hoffert in their east side New York City apartment on August 28, 1963. Robles was held without bail after his court arraignment and on February 16, 1965, he was indicted by the New York County (Manhattan) grand jury for this double murder.

The trial of Richard Robles for the 1963 murders of Janice Wylie and Emily Hoffert began in Manhattan's Supreme Court at 100 Center Street on the second Monday in November 1965. Max Wylie, the father of one of the victims, and Miss Patricia Tolles, who shared the apartment with the victims, testified about their discovery of the crime. The testimony of two police detectives, the first police officers to arrive on the crime scene, identified various items of physical evidence. It was a day of stage-setting in which Prosecutor John Keenan presented a detailed description of the crime scene and its mute evidence of death. Defense counsel John Hoffinger cross-examined each of the witnesses briefly.

The second day of the trial brought more details of the crime scene and testimony about the cause of death. The last witnesses to testify were from the staff of the chief medical examiner. They established the cause of death as multiple stab wounds and set the time of death between 10:00 A.M. and 4:00 P.M. One witness, a pathologist who had examined the undigested contents of the stomachs of the victims, offered an opinion that the time of death was between 10:00 A.M. and 12:00 noon.

FIGURE 9 George Whitmore, Jr. (left) was arrested in the Wylie-Hoffert murders. Richard Robles' arrest for the Wylie-Hoffert murders led to Whitmore's discharge. Robles was convicted of the dual slaying.

Nathan ("Jimmy") Delaney, who was to become the principal witness for the prosecution in the trial, monopolized the trial record during the following days. Delaney enlarged on his original tip to the police that Robles had told him: "Jim, I killed two girls." He testified that he and Robles had been friends for over five years; that Robles had appeared without notice at the Delaney apartment on East 84th Street at about 12:00 noon on the day that the two victims were killed; that Robles told the witness in the presence of Delaney's wife, Marjorie, that he was in trouble and needed help—he said that he had just killed two women. Additionally, Delaney testified to further conversations after that day, which continued up to the day before Robles' arrest.

On cross-examination, Delaney admitted that he had not revealed the statement Robles had made to him on the day of the murders until October 1964—more than a year after the event; and that his revelation to the police was only made after *his own* arrest on suspicion of murder. Delaney also admitted that he had three previous felony convictions and knew that even a conviction for manslaughter in this most recent arrest would require a mandatory life sentence under New York laws; that he had asked the assistant district attorney assigned to the Wylie-Hoffert case for immunity in his own case in exchange for revealing the identity of Robles and the details of Robles' statement to him; and that he had agreed to cooperate in trapping Robles as part of this "deal."

At the close of Thursday's court session, the fourth day of the trial, a non-jury hearing on the admissibility of eavesdropping tapes was conducted by presiding Judge Davidson. At its conclusion, and over defense objections, Judge Davidson ruled that selected extracts of audio tapes made by a police-prosecution team were admissible to support Delaney's testimony.

The tapes were played in court the next day, and they corroborated many portions of Delaney's prior testimony. Although the tapes contained segments damaging to Robles' claim of innocence, they did not contain any outright admissions such as the one Delaney had testified Robles made to him and his wife on the day of the Wylie-Hoffert murders.

Additionally, the tape-recorded Robles-Delaney conversations spelled out the new police theory of the crime: that Robles was an experienced "cat burglar" who could climb walls without apparent footholds, and that he entered the apartment through the kitchen window by reaching upward from a lower service-stairway window and swinging himself out and up about seven feet.

During the second week of the murder trial of Richard Robles, Marjorie Delaney was the first major witness. She testified that she was the wife of Nathan Delaney; that she had known the defendant for a few months longer than her husband; and that she was present when Robles arrived at the Delaney's 84th Street home about noon on August 28, 1963, the day of the murders. Her testimony revealed that she was a former prostitute and a long-time drug user who might be motivated by a desire to save her husband, Nathan Delaney, from a lengthy prison sentence. However, her testimony did corroborate her husband's version of his conversation with Robles on that day.

At the close of her testimony, on cross-examination, Marjorie Delaney testified that she was never told by Robles why he had killed the Wylie girl, but recalled Robles justifying the killing of Miss Hoffert to her because of something the girl had said about her glasses. Robles, she explained, had knocked Miss Hoffert's glasses to the floor in their initial struggle, and the girl said, "Give me my glasses." Later, on direct reexamination by the prosecutor, Mrs. Delaney recalled Robles telling her that just as he was reaching down for the glasses, the girl threatened him, saying: "I want to be able to identify you."

On Thursday of that second week of the trial, the prosecution developed the circumstances of the Robles arrest and his police-station confession. A total of five detectives testified. Cross-examination by defense counsel failed to destroy any of these police witnesses or seriously threaten the credibility of their stories.

George Whitmore, Jr., the wrong man in the Wylie-Hoffert murders was among the first witnesses called to testify for the defense in the Robles trial. The apparent strategy of the defense was to place into evidence a crime theory which had been previously acceptable to the police and prosecutor but which was now in conflict with the Robles prosecution and the theory of the crime it involved. Now, cleared of any complicity in the 88th

Street murders, Whitmore blandly accepted defense attempts to prove his guilt. Counsel for Robles, Jack Hoffinger, led Whitmore through the questions and answers he had given to Assistant District Attorney Peter Koste on the day of his arrest in Brooklyn. Defense Counsel Hoffinger also subpoenaed police witnesses, calling to the stand the two Brooklyn detectives who had secured the preliminary statement of guilt from Whitmore prior to his formal questioning. Both testified to the voluntariness of Whitmore's confession, and their belief in his guilt.

In a reversal of traditional roles, Prosecutor John Keenan sharply cross-examined Whitmore and both of the detectives, in an attempt to destroy them as credible witnesses. The prosecutor's line of questioning intimated that Whitmore had confessed under duress, because of trickery and promises made by his interrogators. Whitmore agreed but the police witnesses denied using any physical force or making any threats. One of the detectives admitted deceiving Whitmore into believing that the two murder victims were still alive by leaving the interrogation room, feigning a telephone call, returning, and telling Whitmore that the two girls had just told him they were not mad at Whitmore.

Toward the close of Richard Robles' trial, defense counsel Jack Hoffinger made his final plea of innocence for his client in his summation of the defense's case. He pointed to the weak points of the prosecution case, and emphasized the defense's evidence. He repeated earlier defense objections to the introduction of electronic eavesdropping evidence, and to the admission of Robles' confession based solely on the unverified story of several detectives, all associates in the investigation.

In his charge to the jury, Judge Irwin Davidson devoted a good deal of his instructions to the problems presented by the defense tactic of calling George Whitmore, Jr., the wrong man originally indicted for the dual murders, as a defense witness. Prosecutor John Keenan had continually objected to the intrusion of the question of Whitmore's guilt or innocence into Robles' trial; and prior to permitting defense counsel to read Whitmore's sixty-one page typed question-and-answer confession, Judge Davidson had instructed the jury that he was allowing its admission into evidence not on the issue of Robles' guilt or innocence, but solely as a test of Whitmore's credibility as a witness in this trial.

At 12:56 P.M., December 1, 1965, the Robles case went to the jury. At 6:51 P.M., the jurors returned to the courtroom and delivered their verdict of guilty to Judge Irwin Davidson. The judge polled the jury and all jurors responded in the affirmative: guilty of murder in the first degree. Judge Davidson thanked the jurors briefly for their work, ordered a presentence report on Robles, and set a date for sentencing the following month.

On January 11, 1966, in Manhattan court, Justice Irwin Davidson sentenced Richard Robles, the convicted killer of Janice Wylie and Emily

Hoffert, to life imprisonment. Given the traditional opportunity to speak in his own behalf by Judge Davidson, Robles denied the killings and said that an innocent man was being sentenced to prison.

QUESTIONS

1. On the facts of this case study is the verdict of guilty in the Robles trial justified by the evidence?

2. A prosecutor's "desperation kit" is described as the production of a witness who will testify to admissions of guilt by a person accused of crime. The witness is usually a person awaiting trial, or one in prison, who is seeking to help lessen a sentence of his own, or to secure an early parole. What are the indications, in this case study, which suggest the possible use of a "desperation kit"?[4] What is the likely motivation of a prosecutor for utilizing such a device to overcome the basic presumption of innocence?

3. Does the fact that the police theory of the crime in the Robles case, in direct contradiction to the earlier police theory that pointed to Whitmore, tend to suggest Robles' innocence?

4. What evidence collected by police, other than Robles' confession, supports the police theory of his guilt in the Wylie-Hoffert murders?

SUMMARY

It is unusual in the history of criminal justice in America to be able to develop two case studies about different defendants on the issues of guilt or innocence for the same crime. While each case study offers a situation for analysis and evaluation on the issue of whether the presumption of

[4]Dr. Sam Sheppard, *Endure and Conquer* (New York: World Publishing, 1966), p 268. The author reports a conversation with his attorney on the eve of his second trial for the murder of his wife. They discussed the possibility of the prosecutor using a "desperation kit" in the forthcoming trial. The technique is described as an "old chestnut" used by prosecutors who cannot make their case any other way, and it involves combing prisons for a willing witness who will come into court and swear to the guilt of the defendant, and testify that the defendant admitted the crime to him.

innocence had been overcome, the two cases together will afford many opportunities for discussing just what evidence was collected to support the confessions made by each defendant. After all, the police never did locate an eyewitness to "place" either defendant at the scene of the crime, and when the origin of the photographs in the Whitmore case was questioned, it highlighted the fact that no physical evidence connected either defendant with either the crime scene or the victims. Discussion sessions can analyze each case on the question of the legal significance of the evidence collected by the police and prosecutor.

Lastly, the theory that there is a procedure known as a "desperation kit" is worthy of extensive analysis and discussion in relation to the assumed safeguard of the presumption of innocence.

CHAPTER SEVEN

Fair Trial

The United States Supreme Court has ruled in the area of pretrial publicity, and has established limits beyond which a person accused of crime might be denied the opportunity of a fair trial because of extensive pretrial news coverage.[1] But little attention has been given to the overall impact that publicity about crime and criminals has on police investigations, and investigation techniques.

Police work often appears to its practitioners to be a frustrating profession in which all the odds favor the criminal. There is a desperate sense of impotence when a policeman cannot find witnesses—a strong feeling of inadequacy when a thorough search of a crime scene uncovers no trace or clue to the criminal. When this is joined with the pressure of pre-solution publicity, it is a natural force for nudging police or prosecutor, or both, into hasty action. When the people and the press express approval of the action taken, there is then an equal pressure to keep the practitioners committed to their precipitate action.

There is also a disturbing pattern in our history of wrong-way criminal cases. This pattern suggests that a fair trial may be jeopardized whenever the suspect in a criminal case is the kind of person the police, the prosecutor, the trial judge, the jury, and, of course, the people and news media think would commit the particular crime invoved.[2] This is a frightening aspect of the administration of justice, and one that needs probing and analysis. The police may go wrong-way now and then at their operation levels and it may be due to their response to news media stories, but

[1]*Sheppard v. Maxwell*, 384 U.S. 333 (1966)
[2]Paul Holmes, *The Sheppard Murder Case* (New York: McKay, 1961), pp. 303–5.

it is only possible for the police mistake to become an injustice when there is some agreement in the community and in other criminal justice agencies that the suspect is the kind of person likely to be guilty of the crime charged.

The two cases in this chapter, Case Studies 17 and 18, offer unusual opportunities to evaluate the potential of prejudicial publicity to ruin a defendant's right to a fair trial. In the first case, the publicity had prejudicial overtones long before the suspects were even identified and arrested. In the second case, the prejudicial publicity not only identified the major suspect before the police arrested him, but it also demanded the arrest long before it was made.[3]

The major issue in these two cases is whether these particular defendants received a fair trial. Of almost equal importance, however, is the capability of the prejudicial publicity to influence people about the certainty of an accused's guilt and thus deny *any* defendant a fair trial.[4] There is no doubt the minds of prospective jurors are influenced as to an accused's guilt by such publicity, but there is also little doubt that such publicity has a similar influence upon police, the prosecutor's staff, judges, and prosecution witnesses. The situations in both cases in this chapter offer excellent opportunities to determine how this influence manifests itself in tending to deny a defendant a fair trial.

[3]Dr. Sam Sheppard, *Endure and Conquer* (New York: World Publishing, 1966), pp. 30–31, 42–44, 79–80.

[4]Frank G. Raichle, "Fair Trial—Free Press," in *Criminological Controversies*, ed. Richard D. Knudten (New York: Appleton-Century-Crofts, 1968), pp. 173–97.

The Verderoza-Lombardozzi Case

This case study is included because of its similarity to the famous Sacco-Vanzetti case, a controversial case in the history of criminal justice in America. Bartolomeo Vanzetti and Nicola Sacco emerged on the American national scene in post-World War I days. They were professed anarchists of Italian birth and foreign appearance who were convicted of an armed robbery and the murder of two payroll guards in 1921 by a Massachusetts court and then sentenced to death. The testimony of a police ballistics expert was the compelling evidence in the case.[5]

As in the Sacco-Vanzetti case, the two defendants in this case study are "radicals." Sacco and Vanzetti were associated with labor—a workingman's movement; the defendants in this case were identified with the campus or student "movement." They have foreign-sounding names, but they are not of foreign birth and appearance. However, their long hair and untidy appearance allows their classification as hippies.

In this case, the police chief, Michael Stewart, and the reporter, Fred Cook, are the main characters in the development of the prejudicial publicity.

The expert in police science, Professor Dimitri Nichanian, assumes the role of narrator divulging the "mechanics" of the trial and the guilty verdict.

There are five scenes in this dramatized case study. The first four move in rapid fashion from the time of the crime to the arrest, the trial and

---

[5]Robert H. Montgomery, *Sacco-Vanzetti: The Murder and the Myth* (New York: Devin-Adair, 1960), pp. 3–22.

FIGURE 10 Nicola Sacco (left) and Bartolomeo Vanzetti were arrested and convicted of a payroll robbery-murder in Massachusetts over fifty years ago. They were foreign-born, confessed radicals, poor and unpopular. They were sentenced to death and executed. In recent years, strong evidence indicates these two men were victims of a colossal community injustice.

conviction. The last scene is really an epilogue which reviews the circumstances of the trial and punishment.

CAST OF CHARACTERS

Police Chief   MICHAEL STEWART: *The chief is about 40 years old, 6-feet tall, and 200 pounds, with gray hair, brown eyes. He has been a policeman for 20 years.*

Reporter   FRED COOK: *Fred is an outgoing person, about 23 years old, 5 feet 8 inches tall, and 180 pounds, with blond hair and blue eyes. He has been a local reporter for 2 years.*

Defendants   ANTHONY VERDEROZA *and* CARMINE LOMBAR-DOZZI: *Both defendants are in their early twenties, wear their hair long, and have been associated with "radical" student groups.*

Expert   PROFESSOR DIMITRI NICHANIAN: *The professor is qualified in the courts of several states as a*

> *firearms and ballistics expert. He is about 60 years old, tall, heavy, and has a lifetime of experience with crime and criminals.*

SCENE 1: *Office of Police Chief. There is a large desk, chair, cabinets, and an American flag on a floor stand. The time is the day after a vicious payroll robbery in which two payroll guards were shot and killed. The scene opens as reporter Fred Cook is interviewing Chief Stewart.*

POLICE CHIEF STEWART: The robbery was plainly an amateur job. A bunch of beginners—and killers more than robbers.

REPORTER: What clues do you have, Chief? Who do you think did it?

POLICE CHIEF STEWART: We have two good items of evidence: some empty cartridge cases, and a good description of the driver of the getaway car.

REPORTER: What are the names of the witnesses? How many people saw the driver? Is it really a good description, or just "a dark man" sort of stuff?

POLICE CHIEF STEWART: Whoaaa— We don't give out the names of witnesses. And, I really shouldn't be talking so much about it, but it is a crime that hasn't focused on any one person yet, I guess— Well— We do have one good witness, no name now, please. He describes the driver of the car as a dirty man, a long-hair—hair down to his shoulders—and dark and dirty-looking. A regular hippie. A young one, not too old.

REPORTER: Like some of the ones down at the lake this summer?

POLICE CHIEF STEWART: Yeah, the drug-abuse type.

REPORTER: What about the car, Chief?

POLICE CHIEF STEWART: We have a fragment of the license number from another witness. Again, no name, please. Just as we suspected, it was a hot car, and they dumped it about a half mile away. We're checking it for fingerprints now.

REPORTER: Any witnesses see them change cars, Chief? You know, you did a good job on that A&P robbery last year when you dug up a witness that took down the license number of the switch car. Remember, he watched them change cars.

POLICE CHIEF STEWART: Fred, I'm happy to be reminded of that one. We did move fast. We will on this one too. I can promise you that. Tell your people that.

REPORTER: (*Holds up microphone to Chief Stewart*) Chief, how about a few words to our folks on Channel 9?

POLICE CHIEF STEWART: (*Into microphone*) This crime is a vicious murder. Neither man was given a chance. They were shot down in cold blood. But— I can promise you—particularly the families of the victims of these vicious robbers and killers—that the police are working day and night. We have a few good leads, and we expect a break in this case at any moment now. Thank you.

REPORTER: Thank you, Chief. (*Holds microphone off to side*) How far can I go?

POLICE CHIEF STEWART: Fred, go as far as you like. I told you what we have.

REPORTER: (*Into microphone*) Chief Stewart has told it like it is. He cannot tell us everything he knows, but I can tell you this: the police have a key witness. They are keeping his identification hidden. He is a man or woman who will go into court and identify these vicious killers. This witness has given the police an excellent description of these men who shoot and kill without warning; and the police are out—as the Chief said, day and night—looking for them. Both of the suspects are said to be foreign-looking. If you see anything suspicious, don't forget, call Channel 9 or Chief Stewart.

POLICE CHIEF STEWART: That's good, Fred, sock it to them.

SCENE 2: *The same office, several days later. Reporter Fred Cook is again interviewing Chief Stewart.*

REPORTER: Chief, I hope I'm not crashing in too early—it's the middle of the night. I don't get going till about 8 A.M. or 9, just don't—

POLICE CHIEF STEWART: That's okay, Fred. I know you have a 7 A.M. broadcast. You're not out of news in this town, are you?

REPORTER: Just about, Chief. The same old warmed-over stuff. What have you got that's new?

POLICE CHIEF STEWART: We've been stopping and frisking a lot of the the hippie types. You know, we had a good description of the driver of that getaway car. We held a couple of them for investigation, and we found a couple of them who were wanted on traffic warrants. Nothing on the robbery-killing, though. It's a tough case. Do you know both guards are dead now? The second one—

REPORTER: (*Interrupting*) I used that this morning. I understand he died without saying a word, tough—

POLICE CHIEF STEWART: We had hoped he would recover, but— Too bad. You know, I'm working on a theory of this crime, and it isn't from the description, but from the *modus operandi*.

REPORTER: That *is* new! That sounds interesting. What have you got, Chief?

POLICE CHIEF STEWART: I think it's a terror outfit, like the people who plant bombs or throw Molotov cocktails and set fires—the rock-throwers. I think it's a group from some outfit like that. Now, just say radicals—no names. I don't want to get involved with any liberal or radical outfit. I think these kids did this robbery to get some money, cash money, for their radical activities—

REPORTER: Hey, Chief, that's real good!

POLICE CHIEF STEWART: Look at it this way: How many payroll robberies do we have in this town? Hundreds of them over the years. Every Friday and Saturday we look for them. But—and this is important—how many come on like gang-busters? Just this last one—boom, boom, shoot-'em-up. Terror—that's what it is—and that's the bomb-thrower's syndrome.

REPORTER: I can sure use that. That's good.

POLICE CHIEF STEWART: When a guy throws a bomb, he doesn't have any regard for human life. No matter who is injured or killed, it gains—in his mind and the minds of his associates—some political purpose. And that's the way it is with this gang-buster style of robbery. Terror—and money to print some of their pornographic underground papers.

REPORTER: How far can I go? Can I say you think the killers are part of an organized protest group robbing payrolls to get some money to finance their radical movement? Can I—?

POLICE CHIEF STEWART: Say the robbers were part of a radical group, getting money for their work of undermining our government. That's what I think.

REPORTER: Good material. What about the car? Any fingerprints?

POLICE CHIEF STEWART: Fred, I can't talk about that. Just say we are still processing the car, and that we have the state police doing the "ident" work.

REPORTER: What about the shells and the bullets—anything?

POLICE CHIEF STEWART: I *can* talk about *that*. The five empty shells we found at the crime scene have been examined in the state police crime lab. You can say this: we will be able to positively identify the guns that fired these shells, when we find the weapons. The bullets have also been examined, but I have to hold up saying anything on the report of this examination.

REPORTER: You need the suspect guns for comparison tests, is that it?

POLICE CHIEF STEWART: I'm going to pin a badge on you, Freddy. You're beginning to think like a cop.

REPORTER: Chief, I gotta run. I'd like to tape a few words, but I left the office in a hurry, and forgot the damn microphone.

POLICE CHIEF STEWART: (*Laughing*) Like a policeman going to work with an empty holster.

SCENE 3:   *A TV broadcasting station. The set is a desk and chair arrangement. A sign reading: "Channel 9—News" is on the background wall. It is noon of the same day.*

REPORTER: This is Fred Cook, your Channel 9 reporter, with your noontime news. I have just interviewed Police Chief Michael Stewart, and this is our leading news item: Chief Stewart believes Friday's payroll robbery and killing was the work of a radical group trying to get money to finance their un-American activities. If Chief Stewart's crime theory is correct, we have a few dangerous radicals at large in our community —shooting indiscriminately, just as if they were throwing bombs. Chief Stewart terms the way these killers shot first on last Friday, without warning to their victims, as typical of a bomb-thrower's syndrome: a total disregard for your life or mine—for anyone's life. Now— Our next item—

SCENE 4:   *Police Chief Stewart's office, two days later. Fred Cook is interviewing Chief Stewart, and taping his comments.*

REPORTER: (*Holding microphone to Chief Stewart*) Go ahead. Tell us all about it. Good work. Boy—

POLICE CHIEF STEWART: (*Into microphone*) As your police chief, I am happy to report that we have arrested two suspects in last week's payroll robbery and murder. Just as we thought, both men are regular hippies, and both of them confess to using all kinds of drugs. Each one of them, at the time of the arrest, was searched and we found an automatic pistol in the possession of each man. Both guns were found to be fully loaded, and both men had extra ammunition for these guns loose in their pockets. Both of these radicals have been warned of their constitutional rights, and neither one of them is doing any talking—but they openly profess their hatred of our American way of life. I cannot tell you any more details about this case for fear of jeopardizing our chances of convicting them later, claiming that they cannot be tried fairly in our community. Let me just give you their names, and the fact that the guns and ammunition we found on them have been sent to the state police criminalistics laboratory for examination. The first is a white male, twenty-three years of age, who has been identified as Anthony Verderoza. The second is also a white male, about twenty-two years of age, who gives his name as Carmine Lombardozzi. We are checking his fingerprints now to make certain of his identity. We are also checking with the state police intelligence unit as to the possible radical activities of both of these major suspects.

REPORTER: (*Into microphone*) Our police did a fine job on Friday's robbery and murder. Here it is only Thursday, less than a week, and they have the case solved. Good work, Chief Stewart. (*Holds microphone to Chief*)

POLICE CHIEF STEWART: (*Into microphone*) Your police worked night and day on this one. I had the theory that radicals were to blame, and that it was a new type of fund-raising and terror activity. My men did the work of investigation. I'm looking forward to an early trial. We have the right men!

REPORTER: (*Into microphone*) Thank you, Chief Stewart. Again, con gratulations on fine police work.

SCENE 5: *Office of a college professor in police science, who specializes in the area of ballistics. There is a comparison microscope on a desk. Nearby shelves and tables are covered with packages and objects with markings or signs:* EVIDENCE, *or* EVIDENCE—DO NOT TOUCH OR HANDLE. *The time is about two years after the robbery-murder, and the trial and conviction of Verderoza and Lombardozzi.*

PROFESSOR NICHANIAN: This case came to me just about a year after the trial and conviction of Verderoza and Lombardozzi. I think I pronounced them correctly. Anyway, these two men were convicted of felony-murder. It was a fighting trial, on both sides. The compelling evidence was the ballistic items: the five empty shells found at the scene of the crime and the spent bullets recovered from the bodies of the two victims of this crime; that is, in relation to the two automatic pistols found on these men when they were arrested.

There was an eyewitness, but the defense tore him apart on cross-examination. He survived, but the physical description of the robbers that he gave the police just after the crime and the actual appearance of each of the defendants was in major conflict. The defense, naturally, used this to attack his in-court identification. Another factor—there wasn't any line-up for this witness to pick the suspects out of a group of similar men. He just went into the police station and picked out the only two handcuffed men in the room. The defense used this to attack his credibility and his in-court identification—and justly so.

My comment on the ballistic evidence—on what appears to have been the key to the conviction in this case—is that I don't like it! That's a simple statement. Why don't I like it? On two major points. Let me expand on both of these points.

First, the expert on ballistics for the prosecution was a self-educated police captain who had less than a high-school education, and who had taught himself the science of identifying suspect firearms from an examination of fired cases and spent bullets. On the other hand, the defense ballistic expert had a graduate degree in the physical sciences. It is true that his expertise with firearms was limited, but it was sufficient. Also, he did bring scientific competency and method to the witness stand. His testimony was in direct conflict with the police-prosecution expert witness. I would say the defense witness qualifies as an expert in ballistics, while I would not qualify the police-prosecution witness as an expert.

Second, I did not like the testimony of the police ballistics expert. Perhaps, I should say I do not believe that the nonspecific words used by the police ballistic expert was fair to the defendants. He would only say that "it was consistent with his examination" that gun number 1 fired one bullet, and ejected two of the empty shells found by police at the crime scene; and that gun number 2 fired the other bullets, and ejected the other shells found at the crime scene. Think about these words for a moment: "It is consistent." The words are meaningless in relation to any scientific theory of probability. Why didn't this police witness say that *these guns did* fire such bullets and eject such shells? On the other hand, the defense expert's testimony was clear, simple, and coherent. He testified that as a result of his tests, it was his exact opinion that neither gun fired *any* of the bullets nor ejected any of the shells found at the crime scene.

These are my two major reasons for suspecting an injustice, or lack of justice, in the Verderoza and Lombardozzi case. Of course, both of the expert witnesses double-talked opposing counsel on cross-examination. Therefore, cross-examination did nothing to disclose the truth. The case went to the jury with this battle of experts placed in their hands.

The role of the expert witness is to serve as the "hired gun" in a criminal case—hired to shoot down the opposing expert. When police collect physical evidence and there is a scientific examination which places a defendant at the scene of a crime, you can expect the state to produce a police expert to link up that evidence. You can also expect the defense to produce a counter-expert. The police expert works for a salary in the crime lab—he is the hired gun of the prosecution. The defense counsel no doubt shops around until he finds an expert who will testify in opposition to the police expert—he is paid a fee and functions as the hired gun of the defense. It is a shameful battle of experts and I think, in this case, it led to a miscarriage of justice.

I would like to confine my report to the transcript of the trial, but I have been asked to comment on the prejudicial publicity in this case, also. This is a difficult area to apply any kind of scientific method. To be prejudicial, the news must meaningfully interfere with a fair trial. Whether the publicity in this case did, in fact, prejudice the accuseds' likelihood of a fair trial is a difficult question.

The publication of the crime theory of "radicals" being the criminals, with robbery-murder as a new form of fund-raising for radical un-

American activity against the government, was due to the operation of a free press. A free press tells people of a community all it can find out about events that take place in the community. Unfortunately, the question I cannot answer is whether this type of news coverage destroyed the defendants' opportunity for a fair trial.

I can say, in a general summing up, that almost everybody concerned in this trial disliked the defendants and never found a good word of any kind to say for them. This is a scientific finding as a result of scanning thousands of words of trial transcript and news coverage. The community was apparently happy with the verdict: we could not find a single dissenting voice in all of our research, except for the defense counsel, student associates of the defendants, and what was termed the "egg-head intellectual group." The defense counsel, and these others, made continued allegations of persecution—that the wrong men were on trial—but not one representative of government, or of the community, joined with them.

I am going to complete my report with this finding: I believe the weight of the scientific evidence was on the side of the defense, *not* the prosecution. I believe this is legally significant and will help the defendants' case on appeal. Whether prejudicial publicity destroyed the defendants' right to a fair trial is a difficult question, but I believe it was prejudicial and shall so report. This, too, should help to strengthen the defendants' appeal case. Now, justice or injustice is up to the Court of Appeals, a forum of learned appellate judges.

QUESTIONS

1. On the facts of the pretrial publicity, and the comment of police scientist Nichanian, did the defendants in this case receive a fair trial?
2. If the testimony of both experts in firearms identification (ballistics) is rejected, would the eyewitness identification alone serve to "place" the defendants at the crime scene?
3. What actions and statements, by both the police and the press in this case study, tend to indicate that pretrial publicity tended to prejudice the defendants' right to a fair trial?

Dr. Samuel and Marilyn Sheppard

At 5:45 A.M., on July 4, 1954, Marilyn Sheppard, the wife of Dr. Samuel Sheppard, was found dead at the Sheppard residence in Bay Village, a suburb of Cleveland, Ohio. She had been beaten to death with some kind of weapon. Initially, press, police, and coroner had focused suspicion on "Doctor Sam" Sheppard, the husband of the victim.

The victim, Marilyn Sheppard, was thirty-one years old, and four months pregnant. She was lying in a pool of blood in one of two twin beds in the upstairs bedroom of her home. There were blood spatters on the floor and walls of the room, and the victim had been beaten about the head and face with a weapon that cut and bruised: a bludgeon or blunt instrument. The victim's pajamas were torn open, her hands were bruised, and the first physician on the scene said that the injuries had made the victim's face almost unrecognizable. No weapon was found at the scene.

Mayor Houk of Bay Village, a friend of the Sheppards, stated that he had received a call from Dr. Sheppard at about 5:50 A.M., asking for help, and that he and his wife dressed and went to the Sheppard home. He estimates their time of arrival at about 6:00 A.M. Finding Dr. Sheppard in a living-room chair, Houk states he asked, "What happened?" Dr. Sheppard responded, "I don't know, but somebody ought to try to do something for Marilyn." Mrs. Houk went up to the bedroom, viewed the victim and the room, and returned downstairs. She told her husband she had found an apparently dead woman, a lot of blood, and that's about all. Mayor Houk immediately called the police and Dr. Richard Sheppard, the brother-in-law of the victim.

At 6:03 A.M., Patrolman Fred Drenkhan received an alarm from

Mayor Houk. He arrived at the scene at 6:15, and called for an ambulance at 6:18.

Dr. Richard Sheppard arrived at 6:20. He examined the victim, and reported to Patrolman Drenkhan that she was dead. The officer notified the Coroner's office and the Cleveland Police Department, asking that "ident" men be sent to help process the crime scene.

Then, Dr. Richard Sheppard examined his brother Sam, and found him to be in shock, with a swollen eye and an injured neck. He ordered him removed to the Bay View Hospital.

Samuel Sheppard told Patrolman Drenkhan, and the others present, that he and his wife had entertained neighbors—Mr. and Mrs. Ahern, who reside in an adjacent residence—at dinner, and in a post-dinner TV-watching session. Dr. Sheppard dozed off while watching TV. The next thing he remembered was his wife crying out. He hurried upstairs to her bedroom, saw a "form" standing next to his wife's bed. They struggled, he and the "form," and he was hit, either by the "form" or from behind by another person, and he passed out. When he came to, he stated, he was on the floor next to his wife's bed. He got up, took her pulse, and "felt that she was gone." He claimed that, then, he went to the room of his son Samuel, Jr., or "Little Sam." Finding him undisturbed, Dr. Sheppard went downstairs, where he observed a "form" running out the door, and he chased it to the lake shore in front of his house. He seized this person, but in a struggle he was knocked out. Upon regaining consciousness, Dr. Sheppard stated he was lying face down at the edge of the lake, half in and half out of the water. He said he returned to his home, went upstairs, checked the pulse on his wife's neck and "determined or thought that she was gone." He returned downstairs and telephoned a neighbor and friend, J. Spencer Houk, local butcher and Mayor of Bay Village, saying: "Spen, get over here quickly. I think they've killed Marilyn!"

Another brother, Dr. Stephen Sheppard, arrived at 6:50 A.M., with his wife Betty. Dr. Samuel Sheppard walked to the station wagon of the Stephen Sheppards, assisted by his two brothers, and sat in the rear seat. They and Dr. Stephen's wife, Betty, departed at 7:30 A.M., for Bay View Hospital.

Dr. Richard Sheppard's wife, Dorothy, arrived at 7:15 A.M., took custody of the victim's son, Samuel, Jr., from patrolman Drenkhan. She and the boy departed at 7:40 A.M., for her residence.

Coroner Samuel Gerber appeared at the scene at 7:30 A.M., and supervised a search of the house and the surrounding area. Photographs were taken of the crime-scene room, and a fingerprint search was conducted. Possible weapons (pieces of pipe, and surgical "wrenches") found in the search of the residence were seized, marked for identification, and transported to the Coroner's office for examination. Robert Schottke, homicide detective of the Cleveland Police Department, arrived at the crime scene, examined the situation, and conferred with Patrolman Drenkhan and Dr. Gerber.

Samuel Sheppard was questioned at Bay View Hospital by Dr. Gerber and Detective Schottke later that day. In summary, this is the story of the events of the morning as Dr. Sam recalled them during that questioning: He was awakened by a call from his wife. He was not certain if he heard the call, or "sensed" it while asleep. He got up from the living-room couch, climbed up the stairs, and entered his and his wife's bedroom, where he saw someone, man or woman, and was struck and knocked out. He came to, went downstairs and saw a burly, bushy-haired prowler. He chased the prowler to the beach in front of the house, and caught him; but in the ensuing struggle at water's edge, he was knocked out. He recovered, and found his feet and legs in the water. He rose and went to the house, where he telephoned for help. He reported his wrist watch missing, and suspected that the prowler took it while he was unconscious in the bedroom or at the beach. He also stated his suspicions about any one of three rejected admirers of his wife, but he refused to disclose their names at that time. In general, Doctor Sam's story of the events at his home on the night of the crime, his discovery of his wife's body, and of the events immediately thereafter were substantially the same as he told police and the coroner on prior occasions.

The police began to organize their investigation. In summary, they had the following leads:

1. *Fingerprints*: Only one fingerprint was found at the crime scene: the thumb-print of Dr. Samuel Sheppard, which was found on the head of the bed in which his wife was found dead. No fingerprints were found in the living room, kitchen, or stairway. All other surfaces appeared to have been wiped clean.

2. *Victim's background*: Several years of disputes with her husband were revealed, and the victim's knowledge of her husband's extramarital activities. Doctor Sam refused to disclose the names of the persons he had described as "rejected suitors" of his wife.

3. *Motive*: The most likely motive seemed either elimination or anger, or both, on the part of Dr. Samuel Sheppard. Investigation disclosed sexual intimacy between Dr. Sheppard and a former hospital technician, Susan Hayes, which had gone on from the time that both had been working at Bay View Hospital, and continued up to the time of the crime. As proof of the relationship, police discovered the gift of a watch by Dr. Sheppard to Susan Hayes.

4. *Wounds*: The victim sustained twenty-seven blows to the head, and the depth of the wounds indicate rage, or motivation to make certain that the victim was dead. (Motivation to kill to avoid being

identified usually indicates that the killer was known to the victim or observed by the victim in good light, so that a future identification is likely if the victim survives.)

5. *Weapon*: No weapon was produced, but blood stains on the pillow, in the opinion of the coroner, Dr. Gerber, suggested that the murder weapon was a surgical instrument.

6. *Opportunity*: Presence at or near the crime scene at or about time of crime was admitted by Dr. Sheppard. Both the police and the subsequent trial defense were unable to produce any identity of the "form" alleged to be present according to the story of Doctor Sam.

All of these leads, in the opinion of the police, pointed to Dr. Samuel Sheppard. The police-prosecutor theory of the crime placed the time of death as between 3:00 and 4:10 A.M. Other time estimates made by police were: 6 seconds to run to the upstairs bedroom from the living room, and 40 seconds to strike 27 blows. Police believed that Sheppard had no less than two hours (from the latest time of death at 4:10 A.M.) to clean up blood traces, dispose of the weapon, and wipe off fingerprints. The police stressed the fact that diligent police work had failed to develop any other suspect; that no other person but Dr. Sheppard and the victim were placed at the crime scene; and that Doctor Sam's injuries might have been self-inflicted, and maximized by the suspect and his physician relatives. Police

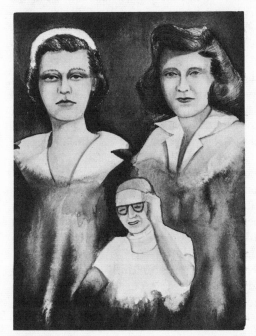

FIGURE 11 The "love triangle" suggested at Dr. Sam Sheppard's trial as motivation for murder: Susan Hayes, the alleged girl-friend (upper left); Marilyn Sheppard, wife and murder victim (upper right); Dr. Sam Sheppard, accused of murdering his wife.

believed that motivation existed for the murder of an unwanted wife, and the existence of Dr. Sheppard's girlfriend was proof that he was having a love affair.

From July 21 to 23, 1954, Dr. Gerber conducted a coroner's inquest. Dr. Samuel Sheppard's counsel was present, but was not allowed to participate. Dr. Gerber ruled that the inquest was an *ex parte* proceeding.

Subsequently, on July 30, 1954, Dr. Samuel Sheppard was arrested for the murder of his wife, Marilyn. He was tried before a jury in the Court of Common Pleas of Cuyahoga County, Ohio. Before the trial began, the defendant was the subject of extensive newspaper, radio, and television publicity, including many matters unfavorable to him that were never presented in court. Publicity was given to charges that Sheppard had purposely impeded the murder investigation, and that he must be guilty since he had hired a prominent criminal lawyer. Wide coverage was also given to claims that Sheppard was a perjurer; that he had sexual relations with numerous women; that his slain wife had characterized him as a "Jekyll-Hyde"; that he was a "bare-faced liar" because of his testimony as to improper police treatment; and, finally, that a woman convict had claimed Sheppard to be the father of her illegitimate child.

The trial-court judge denied numerous requests by the defense counsel for a change of venue. During the nine-week trial, reporters were seated at a press table. Prospective witnesses were interviewd by the news media and, in many instances, they disclosed their expected testimony. The full verbatim testimony of witnesses who had already testified was available in the press to witnesses who had not yet given their own testimony. The trial judge made no effort to control the release of leads, information, and gossip to the press by the prosecuting attorney, the coroner, and police officers.

As the trial progressed, the newspapers summarized and interpreted the evidence, devoting particular attention to the material that incriminated Sheppard, and they often drew unwarranted inferences from testimony. At one point, a front-page picture of Mrs. Sheppard's bloodstained pillow was published after being "doctored" to show more clearly an alleged imprint of a surgical instrument.

After the conclusion of the trial and the wide publicity that accompanied it, Dr. Sheppard was convicted of second-degree murder and sentenced to the Ohio Penitentiary for life.

Sam Sheppard spent the next twelve years in jail; but after a long and arduous appeal process, the verdict in his original trial was vacated, and a new trial was ordered by the court.

Dr. Sam's second trial offers a great deal of information as to the net worth of the evidence presented at his first trial. The new trial began on October 14, 1966. It took a week to select a jury. Defense Counsel F. Lee

Bailey probed the attitudes of prospective jurors with a simple question, "Do you have any opinion of this case which would cause you to have difficulty in according Dr. Sheppard the presumption of innocence to which he is entitled?" The trial judge set up reasonable restrictions which restrained the news media very effectively.

The prosecution case was based on testimony by Detective Schottke; the coroner, Dr. Gerber; and various expert witnesses. The defense in the second trial asked for dismissal as soon as the prosecution completed its case, arguing that no possible motive was developed. Susan Hayes was not a witness, and adultery was not the concern that it had been in the first trial. Moreover, the defense claimed, no evidence linked Sheppard with the crime and its criminal agency. The defense had scored in the cross examination of prosecution witnesses, discrediting a good portion of their direct testimony. They were particularly successful in destroying Dr. Gerber's testimony that the murder bludgeon was a surgical instrument. However, the trial judge ruled that the prosecution had established its case on its merits, he refused to simply dismiss the case and ordered the defense to proceed.

The defense then presented witnesses who testified that Dr. Sheppard's injuries were severe and could not have been self-inflicted or feigned; They also produced witnesses who claimed that a third person had been at the crime scene besides the victim and Dr. Sheppard.

Dr. Paul Leland Kirk, criminalist from the University of California, testified to this third person having the opportunity to commit the murder. He based his testimony on his examination of the crime scene and its blood spots and stains after Sheppard's conviction in 1954 when Dr. Kirk had been retained to get at the truth and possibly develop evidence warranting a new trial. Unheeded in the post-1954 years on motions for a new trial, Dr. Kirk's investigation enabled him to testify and give his opinion as an expert witness that:

1. the killer had positioned himself, or herself, at the foot of the bed on the entrance-door side of the bed for the entire attack (from a study of unbloodied wall areas).

2. the killer was left-handed and swung low, baseball-bat swings, of the bludgeon (from a study of the trajectory of blood traces on walls and floor of the murder scene).

3. the killer had deposited a quantity of his, or her, blood on a closet door (from blood tests and the nature of a large blood spot).

On the question of motive, the defense presented a crime theory during the second trial that denigrated the reputation of the victim, Marilyn

Sheppard. It was alleged that the killer was a jealous woman, probably the wife of a man who was having a love affair with Mrs. Sheppard, or the wife of a man who had acted out such an objective.

Dr. Sheppard was found not guilty in his second trial. Effective control of the press made a fair trial certain. Defense counsel Bailey's successful attack on the major prosecution witness, Dr. Gerber, and the compelling evidence of Dr. Kirk for the defense contributed to the jury's decision to find Dr. Sheppard innocent.[6]

QUESTIONS

1. Was the verdict of guilty in Dr. Samuel Sheppard's first trial justified on the facts of this case study?

2. Do the facts of this case study indicate that Dr. Sheppard had the opportunity for a fair trial at his first trial?

3. Do the facts of the case suggest that it was prejudicial pretrial publicity, or simply an inept defense, that convicted Sam Sheppard at his first trial?

SUMMARY

Publicity about crimes as news events, and other pre-conviction publicity about persons accused of crime, acts as a force for voiding a defendant's opportunity for a fair trial because of its influence on the people of a community, and on the local agents of law enforcement and criminal justice. The major issue in both cases in this chapter is whether the publicity ruined any chance of the accused persons getting a fair trial. The seriousness of this problem is illustrated by the fact that the first case was selected because its facts paralleled a fifty-year-old case now suspected to be a miscarriage of justice. In the second case, the defendant served over twelve years in an Ohio State prison before his first conviction was reversed and a new trial ordered.

[6]Sheppard, *Endure and Conquer*, pp. 297–329.

CHAPTER EIGHT

The Offender

The custody of convicted offenders can be viewed, not only as a form of punishment and deterrent, but also as an opportunity for diagnosis and treatment. Diagnosis and treatment can rehabilitate offenders by altering attitudes and correcting behavior patterns. In this way, custody can be used to reduce the number of offenders in the society.

Longer or shorter periods of confinement in a custodial institution has long been the base for treatment, and the diagnostic techniques of psychology and psychiatry now provide guidelines for programs of treatment likely to help inmates while in custody. An evaluation of an inmate participating in these programs affords an opportunity for staff personnel to predict the time when release on parole can be an effective termination of this treatment.[1]

Failure to grant a timely parole in a meritorious case is not only an injustice, but it is also ineffective management, because the inmate's initiative and drive toward rehabilitation may be destroyed by the denial of the justified parole request. There is a dual moral obligation in the evaluation of an inmate's progress under treatment and the prediction of his future behavior: both the inmate about to be released, and his possible future victims in the community, must be considered. The release of an offender on parole carries a strong message to the parolee—"You are ready." It also transmits a message to the community—"You are safe."

The two cases in this chapter are based on related questions. The first, Case Study 19, asks whether that particular offender should have

---

[1]David Dressler, *Practice and Theory of Probation and Parole*, 2d. ed. (New York: Columbia University Press, 1969), pp. 113–20, 144–58.

been granted parole. The second, Case Study 20, asks whether the offender in the study should have been denied his parole request.

This "parole decision" forces an evaluation of the offender as a person, and of the offender's past behavior. And, above all, it calls for a projection of his likely future behavior. Crime can be studied by examining the criminal behavior of the offender; but these two case studies illustrate that the impact of criminal law on offenders must also be studied. One must consider the impact of law enforcement (what acts are prohibited, and how the law is enforced) and the effect of criminal justice (how the law is administered).[2]

[2]Richard Quinney, *The Social Reality of Crime* (Boston: Little Brown, 1970), pp. 3–25.

Robert Albert Lane

Bob Lane was the adopted son of a thirty-three-year-old commercial telegrapher, Hans Lane, and his twenty-seven-year-old wife. Bob was born on November 2, 1931 in a small town in Illinois, just outside of Chicago. His natural mother and father are unknown. He was very young when he was adopted by the Lanes, and was treated as an only child in a family environment that erred on the side of too much family play and life, rather than too little. Young Bob did well in elementary school, but he dropped out after two years of high school. He then drifted into neighborhood service station work, as do so many other underage job seekers. He began his apprenticeship pumping gasoline, and went on to the work of a garage mechanic, joining the Garage and Service Station Mechanics' Union, Local 705, in Chicago.

In the spring of 1954, Hans Lane was transferred by his employer to New City, a metropolitan center quite distant from Chicago, and young Robert Albert Lane became the operator of a service station selling cut-rate gasoline in New City. But, by June of that year, he was an unemployed young man in a strange city; the service station venture had not proven successful. After three months of seeking work, and some employment as a part-time taxi driver, young Bob enlisted in the U.S. Navy, and was assigned to a downtown harbor installation.

Bob's enlistment in the military may not have been triggered by his inability to secure work, since his parents claimed that he always liked the military. His enlistment may have resulted from a desire to complete his military obligation at a time in his life when he did not seem to be earning a decent salary or to be involved in meaningful work.

In any event, Bob's naval service was uninterrupted for two years, until his arrest on August 24, 1956, for soliciting another male, an eighteen-year-old, for a lewd and indecent act. Bob was imprisoned in the city jail overnight. The next day, on his arraignment, Bob pleaded guilty. On August 27, he was sentenced to pay a fine of $200, and was ordered to register as a convicted sex offender.

The arresting officers found a loaded .38 caliber revolver under the front seat of the car in which the indecent act was committed. It was registered in Bob's name, and he had a legal permit to carry it. The sentencing judge advised Bob to sell the gun, and the chief of the local police had Bob's concealed weapons permit revoked.

When Bob returned to his Navy duties, his conduct on shore was investigated, and he was given an "undesirable" discharge on September 26, 1956. No facts about the discharge are available. Apparently, the circumstances of the arrest alone did not justify this summary and drastic action. It is more than likely that some segments of young Bob's life, known to his supervisors at the harbor installation, were considered as consistent with the main theme of the arrest situation. This data was used to develop a thesis that something was wrong with this sailor that the local representatives of the U.S. Navy believed was beyond their ability to control.

For the next year, Bob pumped gas and fixed cars at a series of service stations and garages. No job lasted longer than two or three months. In December 1957, he applied for, and was accepted as, a Christmas-season employee of the local Sears store, where he impressed the manager of the hardware department. Bob applied for regular employment as a hardware salesman. His application was processed on the recommendation of the department manager, but in the more thorough routine investigation for permanent-job applicants, the record of Bob's registration as a sex offender was disclosed and he was rejected. He went back to pumping gas and fixing cars.

Bob appeared to accept this setback without any emotional turmoil. However, this might have been the event which led to Bob's moving into a small apartment of his own on Turk Street. He told his parents that the daily travel from the Lane home on the outskirts of town to his job in a downtown service station took too much time and that it cost as much as the rent on his downtown "bachelor" apartment. It was a one-room apartment, on the second floor, over a grocery store, but it was within a few blocks of Bob's employment.

Bob lived in the Turk Street apartment through the spring and summer of that year. Then, on September 29, 1958, there came another turning point in the life of Robert Albert Lane. Here are the facts of the event, in the language of the police officer reporting the happening:

Victim is eighteen years old. He was walking along Turk Street when he was stopped in front of number 106 by suspect. Suspect was standing near a car with its engine hood raised, and he asked victim if he would sit in the car and start it for him. Victim complied. After two or three attempts, the car's motor started. Victim was asked by suspect if he wanted a coke and they walked upstairs to the suspect's apartment. After entering and receiving the soft drink, the victim was asked by the suspect to model a bathing suit. The victim refused. The suspect then produced a rifle from a closet, and said to the victim, "I keep this loaded—take off all your clothes." When the victim was undressed, suspect made victim lie on the floor and produced a pair of black-metal handcuffs which he put on the victim. He gave victim an open can of beer and queried him about masturbation. Then suspect made victim masturbate in front of him. Suspect then took off all of his clothes and ordered victim to cooperate if he wanted to go home. Suspect then committed an act of oral copulation on victim, and followed this by ordering victim to do the same act on him. Victim refused, saying, "I'd rather jump out the window first." Suspect began to strike victim with his fists about the body, but stopped when victim began to cry and stated he had to go home. Suspect released victim and allowed him to dress, asking him if he was angry and, if not, could he see him again. The victim, in fear, agreed to a date set for 7:30 P.M. in front of Littleman's Store on Arguello Street. Suspect told victim his name was Bob, walked with him downstairs and up Turk Street to the vicinity of number 200, where suspect left victim, saying they would meet again tomorrow. Victim can identify suspect when seen.

After the victim reported these events to the police, a search of the area was conducted, but the suspect was not found. When the suspect failed to appear for the 7:30 P.M. date, the police began a surveillance of the Turk Street apartment in the hope that the occupant would return. Three days later, Bob turned himself in to the police at the local station near his home. An attorney he had retained was with him at the time, and may have counseled Bob to take this action.

Bob's legal counsel arranged for him to plead guilty to a charge which did not stipulate the use of force, or the display of a firearm. He was sentenced on December 15, 1958, for oral sex perversion on a juvenile. The pre-sentence probation report did not mention the use of force, the prior conviction and $200 fine, or Bob's previous registration as a sex offender. It noted that Bob's family could be supportive, but pointed out this might be a factor in his life that contributed to his unusual behavior. Therefore, it was recommended that Bob be given institutional care, in the hope that treatment during his confinement might help him to cope with his behavior problem, and that confinement until treatment was successful would protect other youngsters such as the victim in this case. The sentence of the court was an indeterminate one, allowing the necessary elasticity for treatment and review: six months to 15 years.

Bob was twenty-seven years old when he arrived at the state prison. He was processed in the same manner as other offenders. The record reveals that Bob claimed to be a nonuser of drugs, but admitted to a moderate use of alcohol with a preference for beer and wine.

As all other offenders, Bob was asked to write an "inmate's version of his crime or problem." Bob Lane wrote:

I think that if I had the required treatment before this happened, it would not have happened. I needed help and did not know who to go to. I had been close to my mother and father, but was afraid to tell them about it. I am sure with the right understanding, I will be able to live a normal life without getting into trouble.

The prison staff prepared detailed reports about Bob, as they do with all new inmates. This "work-up" that the staff did on Bob offers an in-depth review of this young man as an offender and as a person. The following is the actual text of the staff report:

Social Evaluation: This inmate gives the impression of being sincere and cooperative throughout the interview. He admits guilt of his offense, but does not expiate responsibility for it. He repeatedly stated that the victim took an active and voluntary part in the sex act, and that no force or duress was used in any way. He does not deny that he is inclined to homosexual tendencies, and that he has participated in quite a number of sex acts with other males during the past few years. Yet, at this time, he states that he will seek to understand and rectify this type of behavior, and will cooperate with appropriate psychiatric assistance.

The social background of this inmate appears to be close, affectionate, and intact. There are indications that the parents were over-protective, smothering their son with love while setting rigid standards for him. Inmate apparently never severed the parental "apron strings" or developed individuality and maturity for himself.

Inmate identifies with authority, and desires to be liked and accepted by authority. Parole prognosis considered good to outstanding, if inmate acquires insight and understanding in reference to the etiology of his perverse sex habits.

Inmate has average to above-average intelligence. His academic achievement grade is 7.8. He wants to complete high school, and this opportunity should be offered to him. He is uncertain as to vocational training, but believes he may develop interest in learning: (1) office management, (2) accounting, or (3) typing.

This inmate should be transferred to a medium-custody institution with facilities for psychiatric care. He should be assigned to clerical work and to high school classes, with vocational training to begin either at the inmate's request, or on completion of high school classes.

Psychological Evaluation: Intellectual classification of inmate is average, with a capacity above this level. His personality evaluation is character disorder. He employs withdrawal as the chief means of personal defense when faced with anxiety-producing situations. However, the validity of test results may be somewhat jeopardized by inmate's extreme defensiveness and his attempts to appear favorable. Inmate's cultural pattern (Kuder Preference Test) suggests his present difficulty may be found in the effeminacy of identification. Tests indicate that he might act defensively in resisting homosexual advances by other inmates, but the underlying reasons for Lane's homosexuality will have to be explored in psychotherapy.

Diagnostic Impression: Passive-aggressive personality, passive-aggressive type. Psychiatric referral is indicated. Recommended treatment is group psychotherapy, supplemented by individual psychotherapy.

Psychiatric Evaluation: Patient was very sincere during interview. Most of the time his eyes were brimming with tears, as he attempted to impress his sincerity upon the interviewer. He admits guilt to the crime. However, he states that the victim in the crime was a voluntary participant, and no force was applied. Patient states he was first introduced to homosexual practices about three years ago, during his service in the U.S. Navy. Patient appears to be extremely dependent, notably in telling of his experiences as an only child in his parents' home. Because of this, he is unable to compete on an adult level, and he feels confused about his sex identification. While he cannot be considered the "active homosexual partner," there are tendencies in this area which have caused him a great deal of confusion.

Diagnostic Impression: Passive-aggressive personality, passive-dependent type. Lane seemed sincerely motivated for psychiatry, and exposure to therapy will develop data about his response to treatment. He should make a good institutional adjustment, no problem custody-wise; and he should be an active participant in all the programs of the institution.

Custodial Evaluation: This twenty-seven-year-old white inmate gives the impression of wanting to conform to institutional life. Conduct to date has been good. Mail evaluation shows frequent correspondence with friends, but little contact with family. Present offense of sex perversion warrants close observation pending later evaluation. Recommend close custody.

As the staff "work-up" indicates, Robert Albert Lane, now classified as a sex offender, had a rehabilitation program planned for him. While the staff recommendations were to place Bob in medium-custody where he could receive prompt treatment, administrative review resulted in a supplemental recommendation for close custody. This recommendation appeared to be based on the following caution: "Close custody recommended pending observation of need for homosexual segregation. Evaluations did not indicate segregation is required, but in view of inmate's background and present offense, it is best not to be optimistic about this inmate." However, Bob behaved well in the close-custody section. In ninety days he was transferred to medium-custody, and began his treatment program.

In October 1959, not quite a year after he entered prison, Bob made his first appearance before a parole committee. The committee decided to postpone action, scheduled him for a reappearance in six months, to allow time for his treatment and educational programs to be reviewed. In that later review, in March 1960, the parole committee decided on another postponement, this time for one year. Bob was commended for his improvement, and for the promise indicated by the reports of his work in group psychotherapy. His own statement at this time was: "I've learned to think things out before I make a statement. I was wrong in these homosexual tendencies and let my family down. I have been helped to understand myself and the situation is a little better now."

The evaluation of Bob by psychiatric technicians alerted the parole committee to the fact that it was too early to project a date for Bob's release on parole. The psychiatric report read: "Patient asserts group psychotherapy helped him, to some extent, to come to a better understanding of himself. However, inmate's main interest is to get out. He insists he will not become involved with minors in any sexual way, but concedes he is not certain about a possible relationship with an adult male."

On March 28, 1961, Bob Lane's term was set at six years, with the last three years to be on parole status. Since Bob had been committed in December 1958, he would be eligible for parole later that year—about Christmas of 1961.

A program release study, written in December 1961, had this to say about Bob's future parole: "This inmate will live with his father and mother in an upper-middle class neighborhood. His job will be at his employer's needs, part-time, and he will seek steady work elsewhere as soon as possible. Since he will live in a section of the city not serviced by public transportation, he will need a car—his family will arrange this purchase for him. He will report to the local police in accordance with state law, registering as a known sex offender; and he has agreed to avoid contacts with known homosexuals."

Bob was released from state prison to serve the remaining three years of his sentence under parole supervision on December 15, 1961. He left the state prison, went home and the Lane family had their first Christmas together in three years.

A progress report dated March 26, 1962 by Bob's parole officer reveals some change in Bob's living style in the few months following his release on parole. This report states:

> Lane now lives in a small house, having left his parent's home because of his mother's illness and his desire not to make any extra work for her. He is now working for Brown's Furniture, the largest furniture store in the downtown area, and he was very lucky to find this job—although he failed to reveal his parole status to the personnel department at Brown's.

In summary, the case conference reveals Lane is accepting responsibility, and is enterprising in solving his problem. Little is known of his sex life —I presume he practices abstinence. He has few male friends.

Another parole progress report, on June 8, 1962, contained a summary of parole supervision. Additionally, this report noted that Lane had registered as a known sex offender in accordance with state law; had lost the position with Brown's Furniture Store due to not being bondable or because he did not give notice of being a parolee; and was now employed at a service station a few blocks from his residence.

But on June 7, 1962, a day before the above somewhat uneventful parole summary was written, Robert Albert Lane was arrested in New City and charged with kidnapping, robbery, assault with intent to kill, and sex perversion. The local press reported that the victim of this crime was in critical condition from a massive knife wound in his neck, and that if the victim died the charge against Lane would be changed to first-degree murder.

The story of Bob Lane's third arrest began about 5:00 A.M. when a passing motorist found a young man bleeding from a neck wound on a country road at the edge of the city. At the hospital, doctors said it would be a miracle if the youth lived. However, he was able to describe the car of the man who had attacked him, and apparently left him for dead at the side of the road.

Subsequently, Bob Lane was arrested when two policemen on patrol noticed that his car answered the description of the car used in the attempted homicide. A search of Lane's car revealed an identification card belonging to the victim, Carl Gordon, a nineteen-year-old youngster who lived on the outskirts of New City with his parents. Lane was arrested, arraigned in court, held by the magistrate without bail, and assigned legal counsel.

At the time of his arrest, Lane voluntarily submitted to police interrogation. On the night of the crime, June 6, 1962, Lane claimed he had fallen asleep at home, and that he did not awaken until the next day, Thursday. When confronted with the fact of the victim's identification card being found in his automobile, Lane repeated his story of falling asleep at home. When told that the victim's description of the place of attack was a specific description of his home, Lane again repeated his story of falling asleep. However, in this questioning period, Lane admitted he frequently drove about at night and picked up young hitchhikers.

As young Gordon, the victim of the attack, began to recover, detectives were able to interview him in the hospital, and they pieced together these facts: The youth was hitchhiking at the entrance ramp to the freeway in downtown New City at about 11:30 P.M., when a man gave him a ride. But almost immediately, the man pressed a knife against Gordon's side, told him to bend over, and then slipped a looped rope over the young man's wrists, lashing them behind his back. The victim was then driven to a small house, which he described in detail, and forced to take off his clothes. Young Gordon said his hands were retied, and he was then beaten with a strap, made to do fifty or sixty push-ups, fifty or sixty deep knee bends, and then beaten again. The youth said he collapsed on the floor, and the next thing he knew the man who had picked him up was sitting on a nearby couch, and he did not have any clothes on. The man gave him a can of beer, after releasing his hands and threatening to beat him again if he "made any trouble." Then, the man placed the youth on his lap and fondled him sexually. He, then, stretched himself out on the couch and made the youth climb on top of him and embrace him. After that, young Gordon said, the man retied his hands, beat him again with the strap or belt for a few moments, and then began to strike him with his fists, hitting him in the stomach and side. The attacker ordered Gordon to do more push-ups, striking him with the belt when the youth could not do any more.

After what appeared to be only a few moments of rest to young Gordon, he was forced into the bathroom of the house and into the shower stall where his attacker washed some blood from the young man and told him he wouldn't really hurt anyone. Later, under a shower spray of warm

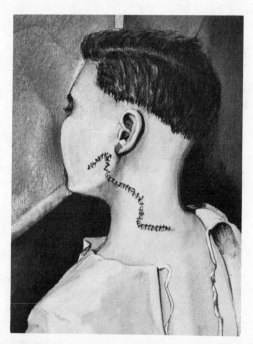

FIGURE 12   The victim who did not die indicates Robert Allen Lane's potential for murder. This 52-stitch neck wound was the result of Lane's knife attack on his last victim.

water, the attacker committed an act of oral copulation on young Gordon and then forced the youth to do the same to him.

Gordon said he was then blindfolded, and he remembers being strangled and not being able to breathe. The youth said he regained consciousness and found that he was in the car, and the man was driving. After about twenty minutes of driving, the man stopped the car at the side of a country road, pressed a knife into young Gordon's side, and ordered him out of the car. The youth said he was knocked down somehow, and the last thing he remembered was the man saying something right into his ear. He believed it was, "Sorry, friend."

After his initial interrogation, Lane signed a waiver of immunity, despite having been assigned legal counsel, and submitted to questioning by the two detectives who had secured the facts of the crime from the victim. He said that he was signing the waiver against legal advice because he wanted to prove now, before the trial, that he was innocent. The detectives found Lane persistent in his denial of any guilt, repeating his story of falling asleep on the night of the crime. He volunteered to take the detectives on a tour of his home to prove it was not the place of the attack.

The detectives accepted Lane's offer, and the subsequent tour was detailed in the police report of the visit. It reads:

Reporting officers accompanied suspect to his home, were admitted by him, and began a search with his consent. The following material was seized and has been marked for identification as evidence in this case:

1. 35 photographs of men and young men, most of them showing nude persons, and some of them showing pornographic poses.
2. 4 photographs of suspect's dog in some lewd pose in contact with suspect's body
·3. 3 leather belts with white metal buckles
4. One 4½-foot length of white clothesline-style rope, with one end looped and the knot taped with black friction tape
5. One memorandum book containing names and telephone numbers.

Lane is also linked with four other homicides. Interviews with assigned police detectives and their supervisors indicate a similar *modus operandi* for all of these killings. Each victim was a young man, a hitchhiker, and each victim had been strangled or had their throats slashed, or both. There is also an expressed belief by investigators that a sex motive was present in these crimes, with the young men being killed either because they resisted abnormal sex advances, or to silence them after such advances. In reviewing the possible link-up of Lane with these crimes, it was found that each crime scene was within reach of his residence or business locations.

Bob Lane's story ended abruptly. While in jail, awaiting trial, he attempted to hang himself from the bars of his cell with a makeshift rope made of strips torn from his clothes. The rope broke, and in the fall Bob's head struck the concrete floor, fracturing his skull and causing a fatal brain injury.

QUESTIONS

1. Was Bob Lane's release on parole justified?
2. Should Lane's parole have been delayed because of the violence involved in his first crime?
3. Did Lane's "good behavior" in prison, and expressed desire to reform, warrant his release on parole?
4. Is it reasonable to expect that proper parole supervision should have discovered Bob Lane's problems prior to the attack on young Gordon?

Thomas MacLean

Thomas MacLean, forty-one years of age, father and husband, and a former user of drugs, is the major character in this case study. Tom is now an inmate of a state prison. He is serving a ten-year sentence for a drug abuse violation, and is awaiting the date when five years of his sentence have been served, and he becomes eligible for parole. The case study is divided into three parts: (1) a criminal history, (2) a social evaluation of Tom's background, and (3) an interview with Tom at State Prison. The first two parts are written in summary style; the interview segment is written in dialogue—just as it was transcribed from the tape-recording of the interview.

CRIMINAL HISTORY

Thomas MacLean was born in Nebraska in 1929. His police record, prior to the arrest for which he is now serving a prison sentence, includes:

YEAR	PLACE	OFFENSE	DISPOSITION
1940	Dallas, Texas	Marijuana Tax Act	None
1942	Dennison, Texas	Runaway juvenile	None
1943	Scottsdale, Ariz.	Bike theft	Dismissed
1947	Grand Island, Neb.	Contributing to the delinquency of a minor	60 days

YEAR	PLACE	OFFENSE	DISPOSITION
1950	Houston, Texas	Possession of Marijuana	6 months (correctional institution)
1952	New Orleans, La.	Possession of Marijuana and furnishing dangerous drugs to minors	5–10 years

The story of Tom's most recent arrest and conviction on the offenses for which he is serving his present sentence began when the police radio, in a certain city, broadcast directions to a police car to go to a location where reportedly a man "was down." As the car was proceeding to the scene, the dispatcher corrected the original message saying: "Man acting suspiciously; juveniles involved." The two police officers, responding to the call, arrived at the scene and found Tom MacLane kneeling at the side of the roadway, looking up to heaven. He was dressed in a sleeveless shirt and dungarees, no hat, and it was raining heavily. The policemen also found three juveniles alongside the road, not far from where Tom was kneeling, a girl of about ten, and two boys about eight and nine. Tom responded to the police queries and readily accepted the police invitation to get in out of the rain—into the police car. He said he was watching the resurrection, and something incoherent about "God in the sky."

The children were more in touch with reality. They told the police where they lived, that Tom was their stepfather, and that they had some experience with drug use themselves.

The police took Tom and the youngsters to their home nearby and met Tom's wife, Dianne. Tom told the police at this time that it was okay to search the house. Police did search, and found a plastic bag of marijuana, and a small quantity of methedrine (speed). They arrested Tom and Dianne and when questioned by police (after being warned of their constitutional rights) Dianne admitted that she and her husband Tom had given the children a puff now and then on a marijuana cigarette, and had also allowed the children to sort the raw pot—seeds and leaves—and were generally "honest" with their children as to their parents' use of pot. The police queried the youngsters and verified these statements. The police took the children to Juvenile Hall to be cared for, and booked the parents on the "possession" and "furnishing" charges. Dianne was Tom's crime partner in the possession of marijuana and dangerous drugs, and in furnishing them to minors (contributing to the delinquency of minors).

Tom and Dianne pleaded guilty to both charges, after Tom negotiated with the prosecutor to secure a light sentence for his wife. His five to ten year indeterminate sentence had a mandatory minimum of five years before he could become eligible for release on parole.

FIGURE 13 Thomas MacLean's "Resurrection in the Sky." Hallucinating from drug abuse, MacLean envisioned a great light in the sky and bodies emerging from the ground.

SOCIAL EVALUATION

Generally, Thomas MacLean had an insecure childhood. He was the youngest of a family of three children and two half brothers (from a previous marriage of his mother). His parents were divorced when Tom was six years old, and Tom spent the school terms with his mother, and his summers with his father. He left school in 1942 when he was thirteen years old and in the eighth grade. At the age of fifteen, he enlisted in the Navy. He was discharged six months later for the convenience of the government, after someone discovered his true age. Tom has a grade placement of 9.7, and his Kuder test reflects interests coinciding with his past employment. He is a bright, normal person with a fair-to-good employment history. He has been married four times.

Tom has a sixteen-year history of drug use, and the hallucinations at the time of his arrest indicates use of hallucinating drugs or mental illness —possibly, both. It appears that because of insecurity and dependency, Tom sought to lose identity through excessive use of drugs.

Tom's own account of his offense is:

> At times, in the past, I gave our children puffs on a marijuana cigarette while smoking myself. I even rolled one or two for them. On the day of my arrest, I didn't know there was anything, any drugs, in the house. I was insane at that time according to two court-appointed psychiatrists, but the jury found me sane at the time of the trial. Actually, they were finding me sane at that time and not at the time of my crime, my arrest day.

INTERVIEW—MACLEAN AND WESTON

WESTON: My name is Paul Weston. This is Tom MacLean. It's all yours, Tom. Tell us something about yourself.

TOM: Well, I got off into the drug bag rather heavily, but I think probably I should back up before going into the details of that. I was born in Nebraska; raised in Missouri; went into the Navy when I was fourteen; became fifteen in the Navy, and was discharged as a result of being underage. I was married at sixteen, the first time and the second time at eighteen and have been married four times altogether. Now, this is certainly a little abnormal, I'm sure. The drug scene came when I was about twenty years old. I was in show business, doing a magic act, and —well let's see—do you want to hear how I first got turned on to drugs?

WESTON: Sure.

TOM: Uh, I was doing a magic act at a club and—

WESTON: This is in the midwest?

TOM: No, this was down south. In between shows I would set up my props for the next show. This particular time I went back into the dressing room to set up my props, and there was a girl getting ready to go on with her number, after my number. And so I smelled this strange smell and said, "Wow, what's that?" And she said, "That's grass, want some?" So I said, "Well, yeah." So I got stoned the first time.

WESTON: What kind of a reaction did you have after the first time you used it?

TOM: I, as I said, was doing a magic act. I went on to my magic act right after having turned on. Wow! I was out there for just about five minutes on stage and it seemed like I had been out there for hours. I did one trick and almost did it again later in the show, forgetting that I had done it. Everything was very distorted and you know, happy and like "so what."

WESTON: How did your drug use progress, or did you stop drug use at that time or after that initial experience or—

TOM: No. As a matter of fact, I liked it, and so the first thing that came to my mind after that was that I wanted to get a supply of this stuff. It was a groovy feeling, you know, it was a lift. It was a "high" that I thought felt better than being drunk on alcohol.

WESTON: How extensive was your use of marijuana?

TOM: I got right off into it. I managed to keep myself with a supply of grass to smoke.

WESTON: How did you do on money? What was the cost of your weekly use?

TOM: Well, grass is not really very expensive. I guess I'd probably smoke a can a week, or something like that, and a can at that time was about ten dollars.

WESTON: You say a "can" a week. It's sort of difficult to get a conception of what a "can" means. How often would you smoke, let's say within a week?

TOM: Every day, every day. I'd get up in the morning. I'd shower and clean up, and I'd smoke a joint. Then I'd go out and have breakfast and do whatever I had to do. After a while, after it was obvious that I was down, why I'd light another joint, and maybe smoke, you know, three or four joints a day at that stage.

WESTON: Being "down"—did it take a while to come down, to lose the effect of the last use of marijuana?

TOM: Three or four hours.

WESTON: About how long after your initial experience did you continue to use grass, marijuana?

TOM: I didn't stop until I was busted and went to the Federal jug the first time. It was a six-months sentence; I did five. I had a month off for good behavior.

WESTON: How old were you at that time?

TOM: Twenty-one or twenty-two.

WESTON: Was that a conviction for possession?

TOM: Yes, it was possession.

WESTON: Did you go back to the use of marijuana when you were released?

TOM: I think it was a psychological addiction. I think that is what it was —anyone would prefer to feel good than to feel bad. Some people have a martini before lunch. I dug the feeling of grass.

WESTON: Was it pretty easy to get a supply?

TOM: Yeah. There's grass most everywhere nowadays. There was then, too.

WESTON: Did the use of the drugs you were using lead to any crime?

TOM: No! No, I didn't do any stealing or any of that stuff.

WESTON: Did you stop using drugs at any time after this period? Did you stop of your own volition, I mean.

TOM: Well now, let's see. I went back to New Orleans, and back into show business, and made the drug scene steady. Smoking grass and so forth. Now, I was busted in New Orleans, and sent to Angola (Louisiana State Prison) for a three-year term. I did one year in the place and did two on parole.

WESTON: Did you go back on marijuana again?

TOM: No. When I got out of Angola, I was paroled into a small town in Arkansas—my brother lived there. I went to work in a shoe store. In fact, I worked my way up to a managership. There just wasn't any drugs available around there. There wasn't any marijuana that I could find. I didn't even really look for it very much.

WESTON: But, it were available, do you think you would have used it?

TOM: I probably would have, yes. If I saw someone that looked pretty hip, I'd strike up a conversation and kind of feel him out to see if he was a weed-head and did turn on.

WESTON: Tom, when did you go back on the use of marijuana?

TOM: About two or three years later. I was transferred from the store in Arkansas to a Milwaukee store. I was manager of the shoe department in a department store there. My assistant manager, believe it or not, was a grass-head and—one thing led to another, I began smoking grass again.

WESTON: Could I get you to tell us about when you first started using something other than grass—the hard narcotics?

TOM: I guess LSD was the next drug I experimented with, and this was some years later, 1964–1965. It was in California. I came to California in 1957.

WESTON: You started to use LSD around 1964 or 1965. Had you ever used any hard drugs before these years?

TOM: I had tried heroin, but I didn't like it. I didn't dig the trip. You'd sit around and scratch and nod, you know. It just wasn't for me.

WESTON: You tried it, but you didn't like it—it didn't grab hold of you, is that it?

TOM: I had a few hits, just to see what it was like. Everybody is saying, "Did you every try any heavy stuff?" I'd say, "No, I never did." They'd say, "Let's try it." So I tried it and I had a few pretty good fixes, but I didn't dig it.

WESTON: How about pills? You know, the—

TOM: Amphetamines? Bennies and so forth? I've taken bennies and I got to shooting crystal, speed, amphetamine, hydrochlorate, or whatever.

WESTON: What kind of business were you in when you began to use acid?

TOM: I was in the radio business at that time. I was doing a jazz show on an FM radio station in the Bay area.

WESTON: How often, Tom, did you use Methedrine?

TOM: I dropped it orally, as a general rule. However, I have taken it intravenously.

WESTON: How often?

TOM: Speed? Now and then. A friend who's dealing grass and acid is also dealing speed. This is the thing about street drugs, you can get more than one thing at the place where you get what you are normally accustomed to. Like if you smoke grass, you'll be at your connection's house one day, and he'll say, "Hey, man, did you ever try any speed?"

WESTON: Tom, did you have any children from any of your marriages?

TOM: Yes! I have a daughter and two sons by my second wife, and a son by my fourth wife. He was born after I was in prison this time.

WESTON: Tom, you mentioned the baby was born after you came to the institution here. Would you tell us the circumstances that brought you here. Was it a crime, burglary or robbery?

TOM: No! No, I was found kneeling beside the road watching the resurrection in the sky. That's how I was arrested. And I was going around knocking on people's doors, telling them this is the last day, this is the day of resurrection. And I was seeing bodies come up out of the ground, and a light in the sky.

WESTON: Did you lose complete touch with everything?

TOM: Completely. I can realize now that you do it so gradually that you're not aware of it at the time that it's happening at all. If it happened very quickly your friends would notice. They'd say, "Man, you're acting awfully weird lately." But, it happens very gradually, and your circle of friends gradually changes. That's another thing, you're off into a different culture, into a different bag entirely. Your new friends are all in that same bag that you're in, and when you say, "Do you see that demon on the limb?" They respond, "Sure thing." They may not see it, but they'll understand that you see it. They think that you really do see it, because they see things too.

WESTON: This began when you started dropping acid?

TOM: Well, after I had been dropping acid a while, after a few trips. When I really blew it was when I got way off into amphetamines, especially speed. Speed is really death.

WESTON: Does speed keep you going?

TOM: Yeah, you can go for three or four days.

WESTON: At the time the policeman picked you up, had you had much sleep?

TOM: I had some sleep the previous night. We had some Methedrine the previous night. Now, the morning that this all happened I didn't have any drugs at all.

WESTON: You didn't have any LSD?

TOM: No, No!

WESTON: Tom, do you think your actions that led to your arrest were the result of the drugs affecting your mind?

TOM: Well, I think this: I probably had some sort of minor psychosis. I didn't know it at the time. Most of the people on the streets and experimenting with drugs do have a few hangups and a little hidden psychosis. These drugs don't help them, they make them worse.

WESTON: If you were just found out in the street how could you end up here? It would seem that you would be more likely to end up in a hospital.

TOM: Here is the way it actually happened. The grass was around the house all the time. Now, maybe some friends and I would be sitting around getting high, passing joints, and one of the kids would come up and say, "Give me a puff on your cigarette, Daddy." So you say, "Well, all right." So he'd go like this (*inhaling*) and then he'd run and play. Now, he really hasn't smoked grass. He hasn't really inhaled it. But, first thing you know, one of your friends talks up, "You don't do it that way—you do it this way (*deep inhalation*)." Now the youngsters, when they take a puff, do it right, and they start getting high. Before too much time has gone by they come up and say, "We want a cigarette of our own." Well, what are you going to do? If you're going to smoke grass in front of everybody, and you're going to say that this is your way of life and that you believe in it, then you're going to give in.

WESTON: When the police took you and your children home, they found drugs in your home?

TOM: The children had a stash that I didn't even know about. Honest to God, they had about a can of grass that I didn't even know they had.

WESTON: How old were these children?

TOM: Nine to eleven years.

WESTON: And they had hidden it?

TOM: They had their own little stash of grass stuffed under the couch cushion.

WESTON: And the police found it?

TOM: Here's the thing: we told our children always to tell the truth. When the youngsters were asked, "Have you any grass in the house?" they brought it out. They told the truth.

WESTON: What about the issue of sanity, your sanity at this time?

TOM: I was found kneeling beside the road, and completely out of it, ranting and raving about the last day. The court appointed two psychiatrists to examine me. Both of these doctors examined me and found me out of it, completely insane at the time they examined me. But, they didn't take me to trial for a few months. They let me sit in jail for a few months and I leveled out a little bit. Then the two psychiatrists came and examined me again. At this time, they said that I was sane enough to stand trial. We went to trial. Our plea was not guilty, and not guilty by reason of insanity, but in talking to my lawyer, I told him, "We've got this sanity issue that both of the court-appointed doctors believe I was insane at the time of the crime." He agreed and we withdrew the not guilty plea. This meant a lesser sentence for Dianne, my wife. This left me with the plea of not guilty by reason of insanity. Both court-appointed doctors testified in my behalf. Then, the prosecution brought in two other doctors who had never even talked to me and by using a hypothetical question, the prosecutor managed to raise a doubt. I had a jury trial on the sanity question, and they found me sane at the time of the crime. They brought in a verdict of "not insane"—that left me with my guilty plea.

WESTON: The sentence was on your plea of guilty?

TOM: Yes, and five to ten years, with five years before I'm eligible for parole. That's in the law, not the idea of the judge. He explained it to me at the sentencing.

WESTON: This brings up a question. You know a lot of people say that the people that use also sell drugs. Did you ever deal in it?

TOM: I dealt in it a little bit, yes.

WESTON: For the money from it or—

TOM: Let's say I would be out of grass, and I don't have much money either. So, I'd get two or three of my friends together and suggest we all go together and score, so that we can get a better deal, a better price. So, they'd give me some money and I'd add my own money and I'd make a buy. I would gather up their money and go to a connection that I knew and get a deal, a pretty good deal. A good enough deal where I could keep a little grass and acid, or crystal, for me and still give my friends their share at a low price and make them happy. To that extent, I'd deal—I was dealing. Now, at one point I was dealing a little heavier than that. I want to be perfectly truthful. At one point, when I had some funds, I would buy ten kilos of grass and give a couple to this guy, and a couple to that guy, and I'd tell them to deal them out and make themselves a few bucks and give me the cost plus a little for expenses.

WESTON: What time period was this dealing with kilos?

TOM: I'd say about a year before my arrest.

WESTON: The last two or three times I spoke to you, about half of it was spent in talking about your future.

TOM: That's where it's at, and here's what I want to do. I want to use this negative aspect, this negative period, shall I say, that I've had to plow through. I'm going to turn it over and use it for a positive. If it is at all possible, I would like to dedicate my time, when I get out of here or even before I get out, to helping other people—to show them the shit I had to go through!

WESTON: I want to thank you, Tom, it's been an experience talking with you.

QUESTIONS

1. Was the conviction and sentence of Tom MacLean justified on the facts of this case study?

2. Is a parent who endangers the health, safety, and morals of a child by furnishing the child dangerous or habit-forming drugs best treated as a criminal, or as a mentally-ill person?

3. Does legislative enactment of mandatory minimum sentences destroy the basic concept of the indeterminate sentence?

4. What circumstances, in this case, justify the lengthy five-year period before parole eligibility?

SUMMARY

These two case studies of offenders are challenging in the scope of each case and the difference between the two offenders as persons and in the situations which sent them to prison. Neither case is intended to be illustrative of any concept of "irresistible impulse" or other drive or motivation.[3] Both cases, however, are intended to show the broad operations of law enforcement and criminal justice by a close viewing of the lives and criminal history of two people. Both offenders are different, but somewhat similar; and the main issue in each case is related but opposed. In Bob Lane's case, the issue is whether his parole was justified. In Tom Mac-Lean's case, the issue is whether his arrest, conviction, and continued confinement is justified?[4]

[3]Jerry L. Simmons, *Deviants* (New York: Glendessary Press, 1969), pp. 50–70.
[4]Lloyd E. Ohlin and Frank J. Remington, "Sentencing Structure: Its Effect Upon Systems for the Administration of Criminal Justice," in *Readings in Criminal Justice*, ed. Jack Ronald Foster (Berkeley, Calif.: McCutchan Publishing, 1969) pp. 279–88.

CHAPTER NINE

Juvenile Justice

Neither the Fourteenth Amendment nor the Bill of Rights is for adults alone. Due process of law is a primary and indispensable foundation of individual freedom, no matter what the age of the offender. A juvenile court hearing on the issue of delinquency must measure up to the essentials of due process and fair treatment, since the juvenile may be subject to the loss of his liberty for years. Moreover, the handling of juveniles, from initial police contact to disposition, involves not only the freedom of the juvenile, but also the parent's right to the custody of their child.[1]

Juvenile court judges are capable of determining the issue of guilt or innocence, and also the selection of alternative plans of action, if guilt is shown. Their choice of remedial programs is based on the juvenile's needs and circumstances, and not on the mere facts of the crime. The juvenile court judge serves a dual role of presiding officer and manager.[2]

Traditionally and theoretically, this failure to grant a youngster the same constitutional safeguards usually given to adults is in a good cause: the welfare of the juvenile. The two cases in this chapter examine the reality of juvenile justice. Case Study 21 examines the procedures used in handling juveniles. Case Study 22 is from the files of a juvenile court. It is about the problem of drug abuse and juvenile crime and delinquency.

The facts given in each case will allow students to evaluate and discuss a new crisis area in law enforcement and criminal justice: juvenile justice—from arrest to disposition.

[1] In re Gault, 387 U.S. 1 (1967).
[2] Edwin M. Lemert, Social Action and Legal Change: Revolution Within the Juvenile Court (Chicago: Aldine, 1970), pp. 182–88.

The Practitioners and the Juveniles

The characters in this case include six professional practitioners, two juveniles—a boy and a girl—and the mother of the boy. The story is told in six scenes and the setting varies from the police station in which an officer is dispatched on the first report of the crime to the juvenile court in which a corrective program is established for the young man in the case study.

CAST OF CHARACTERS

Practitioners   POLICE PATROL OFFICER (*anonymous*)
POLICE DESK SERGEANT (*anonymous*)
PROBATION INTAKE OFFICER (*anonymous*)
PROBATION COUNSELOR (*anonymous*)
PROBATION SUPERVISOR (*anonymous*)
JUVENILE COURT JUDGE (*anonymous*)

Juveniles   WILLIAM MANSFIELD (*boy*)
RONNIE CARP (*girl*)

Parent   MRS. WILLIAM MANSFIELD

SCENE 1: *Police station in a community of 100,000. There is a single desk, several chairs, and a multiple-line telephone. It is late evening.*

DESK SERGEANT: (*To patrol officer standing in front of desk*) Got a job for you. A good one. Keep you out of trouble. On second thought, maybe it will get you in trouble.

PATROL OFFICER: I'm supposed to be working juveniles tonight—But, for you, anything.

DESK SERGEANT: Now I wouldn't work you out of title—juveniles it is. It sounds like an attempted rape. The mother of the girl called.

PATROL OFFICER: Have they, the mother and the girl, got any idea who did it, or who tried to do it? You say "attempted" rape?

DESK SERGEANT: They should have, the boy is an old family friend's son, and an old friend of ours. Here is his juvenile record for you. Listen to this: William Mansfield: loitering, when questioned refused at first to state where he was going. William Mansfield: admits possession of alcohol and intake of two cans of beer. Both cases in the last year, close together, six months ago. Looks like a live one.

PATROL OFFICER: What happened? What was the disposition? Did the Mansfield boy get put on probation on the alcohol rap?

DESK SERGEANT: Nothing, except police reprimand and release. Nothing. Oh! The second one says the kid was uncooperative.

PATROL OFFICER: That's odd. He wouldn't talk on his first contact. He was uncooperative on the second one.

DESK SERGEANT: Go out and take the report from the mother, but try to talk to the girl herself, if you can. If it looks like a decent case, go out and pick up the boy. I'd pick him up and get a statement out of him; then deliver him to Juvenile Hall. I wouldn't even bring him down here. Get the statement out of him in the car, or out at Juvenile Hall. They have a room you can use. Then, leave a request for a continuing investigation report on the offense and someone will interview the mother and girl again tomorrow when they calm down.

PATROL OFFICER: Yes, sir.

SCENE 2: *Same scene, one hour later.*

PATROL OFFICER: (*To Desk Sergeant*) I brought the kid in. He gave me a lot of trouble. Ran away. Took me a half-hour driving around the neighborhood to spot him. Then I had to chase him for about a block.

DESK SERGEANT: Outclassed you, eh? Maybe he's on the high school track team. Where is the kid now?

PATROL OFFICER: I brought him in. He's in the juvenile office. The general story (*reading from notes*) is that the mother claims the Mansfield boy raped her daughter—but after talking to the girl—I don't know. The daughter said that she was down to the park looking for a girl friend when she ran into Bill, that's Mansfield, and they started kidding around near the hot dog stand—it's closed at night—and that Bill got her behind the counter, suddenly exposed himself, knocked her to the floor, tore open her jacket and blouse, pulled down her underpants and tried to rape her—and he pushed her down on the floor, hurting her arms. Sounds hard to believe, though—

DESK SERGEANT: Why is it hard to believe?

PATROL OFFICER: The girl didn't seem too upset about it—

DESK SERGEANT: Was the mother there when you talked to the girl?

PATROL OFFICER: Just at the very beginning—and then as I was leaving.

DESK SERGEANT: What about the boy?

PATROL OFFICER: I found Mansfield at home, but when I told him why I was at his home, he said something about getting a drink of water. I said, "Go ahead." Then I waited and waited. Finally, I realized he'd taken me. He had gone out the back, through the kitchen door. He gave me a bad time, catching him.

DESK SERGEANT: What's his story?

PATROL OFFICER: The kid denies everything. No talk, no statement.

DESK SERGEANT: Don't fool around with him. He's probably too upset to talk. Take him out to Juvenile Hall. Don't waste time. Maybe on the way to the Hall, or out there, he'll give you a statement.

PATROL OFFICER: (*Reluctantly*) I guess you're right.

SCENE 3: *Juvenile hall entrance area. There is a small window set in the hallway wall, apparently opening into an inner office. The time is 30 minutes later.*

PATROL OFFICER: (*Talking into small window set in an office wall*) Got a nasty one for you.

WILLIAM: (*To officer*) I'm sorry about that. I didn't think.

PROBATION INTAKE OFFICER: (*From inside of office*) He doesn't need to be interviewed? You think we ought to keep him out here?

PATROL OFFICER: Sure do. He ran away from me once tonight. No telling where he might run if we send him home, and his mother hasn't been home all night.

PROBATION INTAKE OFFICER: Should I call her? Do you think she'd be willing to come down here?

PATROL OFFICER: Don't waste your time. I tried to reach her just before I drove out here from the station. No answer. Typical—

PROBATION INTAKE OFFICER: What's your name, son? Spell it out for me.

WILLIAM: W-i-l-l-i-a-m, William, M-a-n-s-f-i-e-l-d, Mansfield; and I'm 15—

PROBATION INTAKE OFFICER: We'll get to that. Relax, take it easy. We have all night to go through this. Move down the hall now, I'll open the door.

SCENE 4: *An office in the Juvenile Hall. It contains a desk and two chairs. One chair is for the "boss"; and one chair, for the "subordinate," is alongside of the desk.*

PROBATION SUPERVISOR: Just tell me who authorized releasing the Mansfield boy to the police this morning for the purpose of interrogation?

PROBATION COUNSELOR: It got all fouled up. The boy ran away from the patrol officer who brought him in last night, and then, after he caught him, the officer dumped him out here right away. The intake man noted the boy was uptight. Then, this morning, it seemed reasonable when someone from the police wanted to talk to him—

PROBATION SUPERVISOR: That's not the question I asked. Who authorized it?

PROBATION COUNSELOR: Me, I thought it would be alright.

PROBATION SUPERVISOR: I honestly don't know how you think. Maybe I'm wrong, but once a juvenile is in our custody, we have a responsibility. You know that. I'm wasting time. Have you taken over the case yourself?

PROBATION COUNSELOR: (*Happily*) Sure have, that's to make up— Sure have, and the police were real friendly. They gave me two reports on the boy they didn't have last night—one about an attempted stealing of a bike, and the other about an attempted theft or vandalism from the hot dog stand in the park. Also, they gave me a copy of the Mansfield boy's statement. He gave it to police this morning. I'll read it.

> I was in the park last night about 9:30. I saw a girl I knew—Ronnie something or other—and we started to talk. There were other guys and gals all around, some of them making out, and it got me excited. I walked this girl over to the closed hot dog stand and sat her up on the counter and I stood inside. I was getting more excited and she wasn't fighting. I said, "Let's lay down here." She started acting scared. I think she was kind of crying, and I pulled her down out of sight so no one would see her. I held her until she quieted down. I didn't want to hurt her, just to get her quiet.

PROBATION SUPERVISOR: Don't the police ask questions when they talk to suspects like this?

PROBATION COUNSELOR: Yes— They added that to the boy's statement, here—

PROBATION SUPERVISOR: (*Reading*)

Q. Did you expose yourself?
A. No.
Q. Did you attempt to have intercourse?
A. No.

Q. No attempt at all?

A. Well—I guess I would have if she had wanted to. But— She didn't— She didn't want to.

Q. Did you remove any of the girl's clothing?

A. No. I fooled around with her jacket and under her blouse; and I had my hand— I was pulling on her underpants at one time— But— No, I didn't remove any of her clothing.

Q. Is this a true statement and truthful answers?

A. Yes, they are both true.

Q. You have been warned of your constitutional rights?

A. Yes, I have.

PROBATION COUNSELOR: I'm getting busy today on the family background and I'm going to interview the policeman that the boy ran away from.

PROBATION SUPERVISOR: Okay, and talk to the one who took the statement too. Tell him that once a juvenile is in Juvenile Hall, in our custody, *we* talk to him and *he* doesn't.

PROBATION COUNSELOR: I will— I sure will.

SCENE 5:   *The same office in Juvenile Hall, a day later.*

PROBATION COUNSELOR: I hope you don't mind my busting in. It's about the Mansfield boy, that case—

PROBATION SUPERVISOR: No. Glad to see you in fact. I would have been glad to see you yesterday, too, before you made the decision to release that boy to the police for questioning. Okay (*some change in tone to indicate a willingness to let bygones be bygones*), what's up?

PROBATION COUNSELOR: I called the home of the girl, Ronnie Carp, and spoke to her father. Mr. Carp owns that drugstore down on Thirteenth Street. He told me his wife and daughter were out of town. He said: "They're trying to forget this mess." I hit the roof. I told him that it was his job, and his wife's job, to resolve this problem just as much as it is our job.

PROBATION SUPERVISOR: That's good—and it's true. We're nothing more than parent substitutes.

PROBATION COUNSELOR: It worked, too. He told me to hold the phone, and the mother, Mrs. Carp, came on. She wanted me to go out there, but I told her to come in and bring the girl. They were down here in a half-hour. The girl, Ronnie, she's fifteen. She—I liked her attitude.

PROBATION SUPERVISOR: More than the mother's?

PROBATION COUNSELOR: You can bet on that. Ronnie talked. Her mother didn't stop her. I guess they had it out at home before coming in here. Anyway, Ronnie now tells me that Bill—Mansfield—didn't expose himself, and didn't take her panties down or tear her jacket or blouse.

PROBATION SUPERVISOR: What's left of the case? That knocks out your major complaint, doesn't it?

PROBATION COUNSELOR: Yes and no. The mother claimed that the boy was trying to rape her daughter, and that's what she wants to have on the books. I questioned Ronnie, and she held up on this point: Mansfield, the boy, did pull her arms to get her down on the floor.

PROBATION SUPERVISOR: Did he throw her down? Did he use some meaningful force?

PROBATION COUNSELOR: There is sufficient force, in my opinion, to substantiate a charge of assault and battery. Although Ronnie isn't sure whether the Mansfield boy did pull her down, or if she fell.

PROBATION SUPERVISOR: Have you talked to the police people yet?

PROBATION COUNSELOR: I talked to Lieutenant Arnold in the Juvenile Bureau about changing the referral charge. He's going to insert the change in the girl's statement on their records and reduce the charge from attempted rape to assault and battery.

PROBATION SUPERVISOR: That's good— What have you developed on young Mansfield?

PROBATION COUNSELOR: He seems to be worth working with, there's hope. It's a fatherless home—the father died about two years ago, but the youngster has adjusted to the loss pretty well. Mrs. Mansfield is a dominant woman, no doubt, but there's hope in the real affection between her and the boy. I think we can use this— Now, on the boy, here's a psychodiagnostic evaluation that just came in. The boy was examined yesterday.

PROBATION SUPERVISOR: (*Reading and commenting*) It says: "William denies any attempt to rape, but admits a physical attack on the girl, some use of force, and does not try to place the blame elsewhere. Psychological tests indicate William is not certain about the components of a healthy male-female relationship."

PROBATION COUNSELOR: They mean conflict about the passive-aggressive relationship.

PROBATION SUPERVISOR: They say "components"—that means boy and girl. I hope it still does.

PROBATION COUNSELOR: They mean, I think, that he doesn't know where he should start in this boy-girl business. Ronnie was ready and probably willing up to the last minute. You know how these youngsters talk about "making out."

PROBATION SUPERVISOR: I guess it is a de-escalation from the days of bopping them on the head and dragging them into a cave by the hair. (*Reading again.*) "Psychological findings do not reveal severely aggressive or hostile impulses. The boy is presently dealing with his conflict in a manner that could lead to further aggressive and hostile action toward the opposite sex. The boy's freedom from emotional disorder suggests he can find means, socially approved, of dealing with his conflict." What does that mean?

PROBATION COUNSELOR: Just what it always means. We make the decision. This is the standard jargon for boxing in their examination, but—at least—they have been helpful in telling us the Mansfield boy isn't some kind of a nut—a psycho.

PROBATION SUPERVISOR: Are you filing on the boy?

PROBATION COUNSELOR: Yes, under the circumstances, it seems the best action—to file charges, and bring him to court.

SCENE 6: *A hearing room in Juvenile Court. There is a large rectangular table, and a few chairs. The judge sits on one side against a background of two flags on floor stands. The other characters are on the opposite side of the table. The time is one week after the arrest.*

JUDGE: Do you really think probation is the answer for this Mansfield boy?

PROBATION COUNSELOR: Yes. I don't see how the Youth Authority can help him. He knows what he did is wrong, but he does have a mother willing to help him, and—

JUDGE: (*Looking at papers*) Why didn't she help him before? He's been in trouble: stealing and vandalism, and the vandalism was at the same place as this assault—the hot dog stand in the park. And you know as well as I do that it was an attempted rape. There's also a definite use of force. This assault and battery charge—It should be the old common law: assault with intent to commit a lewd and immoral act.

PROBATION COUNSELOR: The boy admits the assault, but denies that anything else took place. I agree, though, it probably was in his mind, but we can't charge him with that—

JUDGE: It's intent, but I'll let it go— We're getting too technical as it is now. What about the medical report on the girl?

PROBATION COUNSELOR: (*Pointing to papers in the Judge's hand*) There it is. It's by their family doctor, and he just writes: "I find no physical damage from my examination." I called him, but he explained that he didn't want to comment on whether the girl was a virgin. It's weak. But— The girl's story and the boy's statement both agree: there was no sex act.

JUDGE: This doctor doesn't say that. Sure there have been some rapes, some so-called rapes, where it is possible to have a sex act without what this doctor calls "physical damage," but—

MRS. MANSFIELD: (*Walking in*) Is this—?

PROBATION COUNSELOR: (*To Mrs. Mansfield*) Please sit right here. Bill (*to young Mansfield*), sit right here.

JUDGE: Mrs. Mansfield, and you, William—we met at William's detention hearing. At that time, I explained the objectives and purposes of our juvenile court system. Therefore, I think we can get right down to business. This is a hearing on the guilt or innocence of William Mansfield. I'll have the petition now, if you please, Counselor.

PROBATION COUNSELOR: (*Reading*) William Mansfield, a person of the age of fifteen, coming within the provisions of the Health and Juvenile Code of this state, did on July 12, this year, within this city and this county, wilfully and unlawfully use force and violence upon the person of another person, one Ronnie Carp, also a person coming within the provisions of the above law in that she is fifteen years of age, in violation of Section 200 of the Penal Law of this state.

JUDGE: (*To Mrs. Mansfield*) Do you have anything to say now?

MRS. MANSFIELD: Yes! Why did you keep my son in that horrible Juvenile Hall with all those ruffians when he could have been home with me?

JUDGE: Mrs. Mansfield, I had hoped that we had made that perfectly clear at the time of the detention hearing. Your son was, in my judgment, accused of a very serious offense. His act was that of an aggressive person. I made the decision to detain him because of this aggression and, legally speaking, it was a matter of immediate and urgent necessity for the protection of the person or property of another to detain your son. Additionally, your son ran away from the police officer who came to your home to question him about his offense, and it was my decision that he was likely to flee from the jurisdiction of the court. Is that so unreasonable that you cannot understand it?

MRS. MANSFIELD: You know the girl is just as guilty as my son, and even more so—but she wasn't held in Juvenile Hall. Don't tell me that you're so lily-white here in these courts that you don't know the difference between rape and entrapment—

JUDGE: The better comparison would be seduction and rape. No, we are no different here, because of our work with youngsters, than you or your late husband. In fact, the court operates as a form of extended parental control. Please, Mrs. Mansfield, try to understand that William was not hurt by his stay in Juvenile Hall. In fact, our probation people took the opportunity to get to know your son better. Shall we go on?

MRS. MANSFIELD: I don't see why the girl isn't here, just as my son is here.

JUDGE: We have the young lady available. She will be sworn in as a witness if that is necessary. However, if you will—we can deal with that matter later. Let's start at the beginning. Will you (*to counselor*) read the psychodiagnostic report?

PROBATION COUNSELOR: I read it to Mrs. Mansfield in the hallway, just a few minutes ago. She knows how it reads, and William does too—he listened.

JUDGE: (*To Mrs. Mansfield and William*) This report was read to you?

MRS. MANSFIELD: Yes, it was. And I read it over his shoulder as he was reading.

JUDGE: You understand it?

MRS. MANSFIELD: Not completely—it's kind of strangely worded.

JUDGE: Truthfully, it isn't much help. It does indicate your son might, or might not, be aggressive toward females in the future—

MRS. MANSFIELD: You know (*choked up*) that—that—

JUDGE: Don't get excited. This is true of any red-blooded boy of your son's age. It applies to most men, too. Now (*to William*), do you realize you could have seriously injured this girl?

WILLIAM: (*Nods.*)

MRS. MANSFIELD: He does. Yes, he does. He knows that.

JUDGE: (*Again to William*) I hope you realize that any use of force or violence in these sex—these lovemaking situations—can have serious consequences for you, young man. Do you realize that?

WILLIAM: (*Nods.*)

MRS. MANSFIELD: He does. Bill does realize this. I think my son has more of a sense of remorse, or regret, than this girl—

JUDGE: That's fine. Then, is it true that your son admits to this use of force and violence against Miss Ronnie Carp?

WILLIAM: (*Nods.*)

JUDGE: Speak up.

WILLIAM: Yes. It is true.

MRS. MANSFIELD: Yes, that is true. He did take her by the arms and he is sorry for it.

WILLIAM: Yes, I did. I mean, I do admit it.

JUDGE: Then, there is no need to bring in the young lady as a witness to be sworn in and to testify to the force and violence used.

PROBATION COUNSELOR: I don't think so.

JUDGE: (*To William*) The probation office has recommended that I make you a ward of the court, and place you on probation so that you can recover from this experience at home, under the care and supervision of your mother. But— I hesitate—

MRS. MANSFIELD: Please don't hesitate. You will not have to worry about Bill again. I'm going to make certain that I'm home more, and I'll do my best—and Bill is going to do his best.

JUDGE: No juvenile court in the nation could ask for more than that. I hereby so find.

MRS. MANSFIELD: This may be the best thing for Bill.

JUDGE: (*To Counselor*) I'm going to stipulate on this petition that I want William brought back here in— at the end of one year, and (*to Mrs. Mansfield and William*) if Bill stays out of trouble and does well in school, I'm going to terminate his probation.

MRS. MANSFIELD: Thank you. I don't think he'll be any more trouble for anyone.

JUDGE: The burden is on you, young man. Our decision has been to work with you—to help. But *your* decision has to be to work with *us*, and not take any actions that may spoil your chances for a decent career, a good job. Now (*to probation counselor*), let's move on to our next case.

QUESTIONS

1. Did the Mansfield boy receive a fair judicial hearing on the issue of his guilt or innocence?

2. Was the best interests of the juvenile the major factor in the decision to release him to the custody of his mother?

3. Was the police referral of the Mansfield boy to the probation department justified?

4. Was the probation department's decision to file a petition on the Mansfield boy, and thus bring him into juvenile court, justified?

5. Were the constitutional rights of the juvenile in this case violated by police questioning?

The Juvenile Drug Abuser

Richard Harris was born on March 31, 1952. He was called Dickie by his parents, and Dick by his school chums. The case study reveals that as a young man, he became involved with the use of drugs, and slipped into a pattern of criminal behavior. Perhaps Richard's story can best be told by presenting summaries and extracts from the many reports and records that various authorities compiled about him. Taken together, they tell the story of a young man who sinks deeper and deeper into trouble.

The story begins with Richard's records at school. Richard had been doing well at school, and then, suddenly, in High School, he began to get into difficulty. It was a radical change in his behavior pattern. This is the school report about Richard as of October 18, 1966, when he was fourteen:

> Guidance Counselor Adams requested this hearing as a result of Richard's habitual truancy and defiance of school rules. The problem primarily seems to be inability on the part of the school to control Richard's attendance (truancy and "getting lost" between classes). Richard has been truant ten times since September 14 (the last thirty days). This is especially unfortunate since the records show Richard can do the work and, in fact, has been fairly successful considering his atrocious attendance. Therefore, because of Richard's three-year record of truancies, I am requesting that the probation office file a petition in juvenile court.

The petition was filed, and the juvenile court judge's decision was that Richard should be declared a ward of the court, but that he would live at home with his parents, and—under probation supervision—try to correct his school attendance and general behavior pattern. Richard's father was a hard-working laborer and welder, with a good history of employment. His mother added to the family income by working downtown as a lunch-hour waitress. They wanted Richard to remain at home, and the juvenile court judge believed that this home life, plus professional supervision by the county probation office, would be ideal for Richard.

In a chronological development of the life history of this youngster, the next item is dated February 1967, and concerns an incident in Richard's life that happened six months earlier, in September 1966—during the ten-days-out-of-thirty pattern of Richard's truancy mentioned by his school guidance counselor. This incident concerns the local U.S. District courtroom. It is a case of vandalism—a strange case. The courthouse janitor found the desk blotter on the judge's desk rudely marked up: "Hello, Judge. I find you guilty—you put my father to death. Now I'm going to kill you, Judge. Goodby Judge. I mean it, Judge. His son, Richard."

The courthouse janitor also found that a ballpoint pen had been used to scar out on the counter-top of the judge's bench this message: "Goodby Judge—Goodby Judge—see you in the morgue, Judge."

There was some additional writing on a blackboard near the court's jury box. Some of it was obscene, some jumbled, but it ended nice and clear—as if the writer was proud of his composition: "Hi, Richard Harris was here in '66."

Originally, the Federal District Attorney filed for prosecution under Title 18, Section 1503, Obstruction of Justice. An FBI handwriting expert was called in, and he examined samples of Richard's handwriting secured from his school, and stated that the courtroom threats and obscenities appeared to be in Richard's handwriting. However, since Richard was a ward of the juvenile court in the county, the case was not pursued at the federal level.

Throughout the year 1967, the probation officer kept close watch over Richard, and filed detailed reports. Some of the items contained were:

1. Decayed teeth fixed by family.
2. Father drinking: appeared out of kitchen at end of home visit interview (to the apparent embarrassment of Richard and his mother) and bragged about being "rid" of school early—dropping out in the 7th or 8th grade and hiding from "truant officers." He blamed the school for not "keeping" his son in classes.
3. Mother now unemployed; applied for disability funds.
4. Richard makes no effort to seek help. Once he took the bus to Youth Opportunity Center to look for summer or after-school work. He got off at the wrong stop and then went home, making no effort to find the Youth Opportunity Center.
5. Richard reports that because of his past use of acid, he occasionally gets a really strong reaction from marijuana.

On March 8, 1968, another type of report, an Acceptance Into Custody Report, was filed about Richard. It reads:

> Juvenile advised of rights and waived. Juvenile truant part or all day thirty-five times and absent on forty-eight other occasions in school year. He was suspended from school three times this year—last time from February 29 to March 7 (yesterday). Juvenile uses obscene language in class and constantly defies school rules.

In early 1968, the school authorities tried various means to get Richard to attend (notices to his parents, counseling in the school guidance office, etc.), but when he didn't come to school until late in the day on March 8, after a week's suspension for truancy, the school authorities again sought the help of the Probation Department.

There is another Acceptance of Custody Report on Richard. It lists him as a truant and states:

> On May 27, 1968 (yesterday) minor was informed at a school supervisor's conference, attended by himself and his probation officer, that if he cut classes or was late again, a petition would be filed. On May 28, 1968 (today), minor, knowing his high school has a closed campus. left school to go to a nearby store and was missing from school for twenty minutes. On May 22, 23, and 24, 1968 (last week), minor had nine cuts, his only class attendance without a cut was P.E. The disposition of this truancy case at this time was to counsel Richard and keep him in the custody of his parents; but to increase the probation supervision, to give the assigned probation officer an opportunity to work with the minor.

Six months later, in October 1968, Richard was again cited for truancy by his probation officer. The report states: "Minor is an inexplicable truant for the past three years. He has been truant nineteen days between September 14 and October 18 (last week), and after a hearing at school about his conduct on October 18, minor was truant or partially truant on October 19, 20, and 21." The report also contains Richard's views about his situation.

> Minor readily admits truancies, stating he is a 'follower,' and that he has been truant with Joe Costello, and Bruce Gonzalez; and that he plays pool at the Rainbow Bowling Alley, or stays at home when truant. Minor claims C-average in school, with an F in gym, because he is often absent and fails to 'dress out.' States he guesses he can go to school, gives no reason for truancies.

The report concludes with a brief review of Richard's home life:

> Minor now lives with mother, father and sixteen-year-old brother, and he has two older brothers, one, twenty years old, in the U.S. Air Force,

the other nineteen years of age, in the U.S. Navy. Mother admits hiding certain behavior of Richard's from father. She did not tell him of the October hearing at school on Richard's continued truancy.

Richard's school record at this time—believe it or not—does reveal a C-average, with the only F on record in physical education. Placed alongside of his attendance record, it is unbelievable.

So, while he was in high school, Richard's truancy led to a deep embroilment with the school authorities and the probation agency, although none of their efforts succeeded. Then, in February 1970, four months after his last school hearing, Richard established contact with a different agency —the police.

The police took Richard into custody for receiving stolen property. The police offense report is not too clear, and the police case is not too well developed. But, it does seem to indicate that after there were several burglaries of antique stores in Richard's home area and there had been attempts to sell some old bottles stolen in the burglaries, the police picked up Richard and put him in a lineup. Richard was picked out of this lineup of suspects by an antique dealer who said that two boys tried to sell him stolen articles. Richard denied the man's claim, and said that he knew nothing of the property stolen, or the attempts to sell it.

At this time, February 1970, Richard lived with his mother. His parents had been legally separated for two months. Richard's mother defended him, and the police dropped the case for lack of evidence when Richard continued to claim innocence.

Two weeks later, on February 22, 1970, Richard's probation officer noted that Richard was on drugs. The probation officer's report reads:

> Visited residence of Richard Harris at call of mother. Mother and brother searched ward's room and found miscellaneous pills and physician's samples. Ward admits he had shot Thorazine. Ward's arm "tracked" above and below the elbow. Ward's statement: "I dropped two reds last night and shot half a cc of Thorazine. I paid three dollars for the reds and four dollars for the other drugs, and I got them right around where I live— but I don't know the boy's name." Ward admits to the use of Methedrine once or twice a week since last Fall.

This time Richard's mother asked for help. She said, "Don't release him, he has a severe drug problem, I need help with him." At a detention hearing in juvenile court, that followed this report, the judge ordered that Richard be detained at the Juvenile Center. At that time, the local probation people did an extensive work-up on him. It is dated February 26, 1970, and is a professional psychological evaluation:

> Minor "Dick" was previously seen in February 1967. At this time he is emotionally unexpressive, unanimated, and very slow-spoken. He seems

reasonably well-oriented with relevant responses to questions, yet verbalizations were typically brief and vague. He says he is ready to cooperate, but he is disinterested, unmoved or preoccupied.

Regarding his drug use, Dick explains that he started using drugs in about 1967, and he stopped when he was in Juvenile Center in 1968 because of his truancies, but began again immediately upon release. Then, he stopped using after a few months or a year, primarily because "acid" caused him to freak out. He soon resumed using marijuana and drugs, primarily because he became acquainted again with some old "narco" friends. He stated that in recent months he has had a very expensive habit. Also, that "speed" makes him skinny and dehydrated, and that before his arrest he intended to quit. In fact, Dick states that his present trouble began when he told his mother of the drugs, and of his desire to receive some type of treatment.

Two tests were administered to Dick. They were the BG (Bender-Gestalt) and the DAP (Draw-a-Person). The significant test findings were: ward has ability to handle situations, but this ability is a bit faulty. The heads drawn in the DAP test resembled manikins, and this might say something about the poverty of Richard's interpersonal life.

The summary and conclusions of this report were:

Dick is a very thin, emaciated-looking seventeen-year-old boy, with wild hair and a generally disheveled appearance, who admits to long-term use of drugs, with a serious drug habit for the past year, and who now maintains he wants to quit. There is a faulty family relationship, which seems to have contributed to this boy's apparent lack of any sense of security or personal adequacy, and he views people, especially those in authority, as ungiving and undependable. He has probably developed failure expectations about conventionally competing with others for acceptance or approval, and in such a demoralized boy, drug abuse is not surprising.

At this point in Richard's life, he seems uncertain to the point of lethargy, emotionally flat, and without any particular purpose or direction. He does not seem to know what he wants to do with his life, or what he has been doing with his life other than "trying to get drugs." Yet, he states with an air of confidence that he definitely intends to stop using drugs.

This examiner is not quite as confident as Dick about his intention to stop using drugs; however, a return to his home may be worth a try—providing he can definitely be placed in an out-patient treatment program with additional supervision by a probation officer who may be able to supply Dick with the structure and encouragement he needs. Otherwise, the outlook at this point is not too promising, and treatment of Dick in a boy's school with clinical facilities may be advisable until he reaches the age of 18.

At the Juvenile Court hearing, the probation officer assigned to Richard's case based his recommendation mainly on the psychological evaluation of this juvenile. The recommendation was that he be released, but to the care and custody of his older brother, who was now back from the Air Force, was married, childless, and living some distance from the mother's home. The judge ruled in accordance with the probation recommendation. Richard was kept as a ward, but released. He went to live with his brother who, the court believed, would supply the necessary structure to Richard's life and who could give him encouragement to change.

An interesting part of this program of the court for Richard was a requirement that he work weekends in the city parks on a juvenile work program. The reports from his supervisor on this project illustrate Richard's attitude toward authority. The first report is dated March 1970, the first weekend after Richard's release to his brother's care and custody. It reads: "Minor refused to work, saying he was sick; no credit for day." The next one reads: "Minor did not report for work, allegedly sick at home—no credit for day." Another, the next weekend, reads: "Minor asked to sit in the bus. Refused by supervisor, who did not think minor was ill. This minor is somewhat of a management problem, and has received poor grades; he does not accept supervision."

Less than two months later, the police again picked up Richard Harris—this time, as a burglar. And this time the police report was clear, and it presented an excellent case. Richard even admits to the excellence of the police work. The police, upon arrival at a reported burglary scene outside of a doctor's office, found Richard by a broken window with black socks on his hands. Briefly, the substance of the report is: Dick said to the police, "Guess you caught me this time." Then, after being given the Miranda warning about his rights, Dick told the police: (a) "I used a bolt to break the window"; (b) "I wore the socks to hide my fingerprints"; (c) "I threw the bolt away after using it, it's over there" (recovered by police); and (d) "I'm a drug user—marijuana and 'speed' the last few months."

Police detectives say Dick is known to have committed three burglaries:

1. January 3, 1970, at the Christian Gospel Church, taking jewelry, a guitar, a radio, and a roll of stamps
2. January 15, 1970, at the Free Christian Church, taking an amplifier and P. A. system
3. Kelly and Schwartz Realty Office, taking a tape recorder, an adding machine, and a man's jacket.

After the burglary arrest, Richard was again scheduled to appear in Juvenile Court—his sixth appearance. This time it was for burglary of the doctor's office and two other burglaries. In this latest conflict between Richard and the police, he readily admitted his guilt.

In a foreshadowing of the action of the Juvenile Court, the probation officer concluded his petition with these words:

No further resources available within the family nor through the probation department to satisfactorily handle this minor's numerous problems. No alternative but commitment to the Youth Authority.

Because the petition alleges an act of delinquency that would have been a crime if committed by an adult, a member of the staff of the public defender was assigned to the case. He conferred with Richard and his mother at the detention hearing, and informed the court of the mother's belief that the boy would go back to drug use if released. The court ordered Richard to be held at the juvenile center pending a hearing on guilt or innocence.

At the Juvenile Court hearing on the merits of the police case, the investigating detectives were available and testified to the facts of the case, including the minor's admission of guilt. Richard's counsel stipulated that the facts were substantially as related, but pleaded that Richard's drug addiction was a controlling factor in his conduct, and that he should be treated as a sick person rather than a delinquent. After conferring with Richard and his brother, the juvenile court judge ordered that Richard be committed to the state institutional program for juveniles as a ward of the county. Richard had gone from truancy, to drugs, to burglary, and, finally, he had to be placed in correctional custody.

QUESTIONS

1. Was Richard Harris's right to due process protected during his last juvenile court hearing on the merits of the police case on the burglary charge?

2. Is the relationship between drug abuse and crime so intimately related that the abuse of illegal drugs, in effect, excuses crime or lessens the concept of criminal responsibility?

3. Did the assistance of legal counsel, and the safeguards of due process, have any significant influence on the outcome of this case?

4. Throughout this case study, was the action taken by the practitioners (police, probation authorities, and the court) in the best interests of the juvenile?

5. Would Richard, and the community, have been better served if he would have been put directly in an institution—instead of on probation—when his drug use was discovered?

SUMMARY

The control of juvenile delinquency confronts practitioners in this field with difficult and complex problems. Juvenile justice involves more than boys and girls who tangle with the law. It is law enforcement and criminal justice at a time in a person's life when the right program of help and re-habilitation can reward all the interested persons: the youngster and his parents, the practitioners concerned, and the community.

The main issue of the two cases in this chapter is whether the young-sters in these studies received all the protection of the Constitution. How-ever, inherent in any review of juvenile justice is a question greater than "due process." This is whether the actions taken in each of these case studies were in the best interest of William Mansfield and Richard Harris —the two juveniles in the case studies.

SELECTED
BIBLIOGRAPHY

DRESSLER, DAVID. *Practice and Theory in Probation and Parole*. 2d ed. New York: Columbia University Press, 1969.

The story of "where we stand and what we are about in probation and parole."

LAFAVE, WAYNE R. *Arrest: The Decision to Take a Suspect Into Custody*. Boston, Mass.: Little, Brown and Co., 1965.

The report of the American Bar Foundation's Survey of the Administration of Criminal Justice in the United States. An examination of current police and criminal justice practices relating to the decision to arrest, and the critical problems of the apprehension process.

LANE, ROGER. *Policing the City: Boston 1822–1885*. Cambridge, Mass.: Harvard University Press, 1967.

A scholarly history of the evolution of the professional police in nineteenth-century Boston. Boston's problems were similar to those of other urban centers at this time, and the Boston story is typical of the evolution of American policing.

MARTIN, RALPH G. *The Bosses*. New York: G. P. Putnam's Sons, 1964.

A story of political power in America: the inside stories of graft and corruption in "machine" politics.

QUINNEY, RICHARD. *The Social Reality of Crime*. Boston: Little, Brown, 1970.

A study of criminology with a new relevancy to our times and emerging concepts of justice and individual freedom; new horizons in criminal definitions and the related development of behavior patterns.

SMITH, BRUCE. *Police Systems in the United States*. 2d rev. ed. New York: Harper & Row, 1960.

Bruce Smith, Jr., has edited and updated his father's classic 1940 text on the American "non-system" of policing.

WILSON, JAMES Q. *Varieties of Police Behavior*. Cambridge, Mass.: Harvard University Press, 1969.

A book about how police are governed. Three "styles" of local policing (watchman, service, and legalistic) are examined in their relationships to local and regional politics.

WESTON, PAUL B. and WELLS, KENNETH M. *Criminal Investigation: Basic Perspectives*. Englewood Cliffs, N.J.: Prentice-Hall, 1970.

A detailed development of a system of criminal investigation.

Case Index

Index